High Shelf

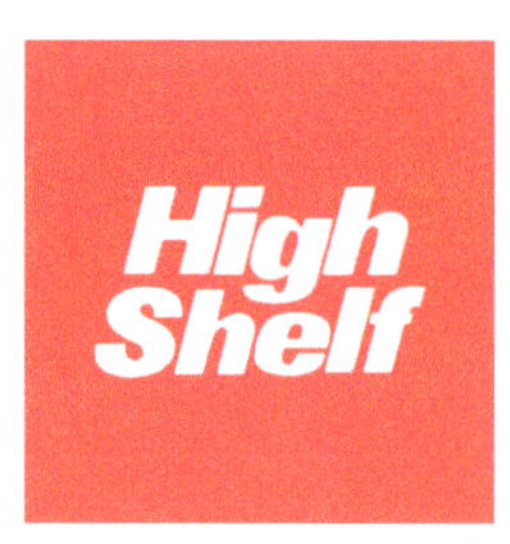

High Shelf XXIX. April 2021.
Portland, Oregon.
Copyright 2021, High Shelf Press

ISBN: 978-1-952869-29-7

Cover Image by Martha Clarkson
Design, Layout, and Editing by C. M. Tollefson

With special thanks to:
David Seung, Megan Kim, River Elizabeth Hall, & Eric Hoskins.

High Shelf XXIX

April 2021

"... its value lost
on me today
the joy of getting melts
the misery of having..."

Heather Gluck

"... Then the waiting and the waiting and the waiting.
Now, we wait again. ..."
Beth Curran

Table Of Contents

Become a Writer

Tom Halford

Submit short-stories to literary
magazines. Get a few published, and then
you're a known entity, after that then
you go local, and send out your first book,
to an award winning regional press.

You need an author photo like Camus,
the coolest brain, maybe you could smile
ironically, but don't let your teeth
show. People might assume you are happy.
Look a little tired, slouch, and imply
a prolonged sadness with your left eyebrow.
Happy people don't write interesting
books. People with flat smiles write the best books.

Then wake the people who
have the same dream as you
and laugh together. Laugh
at the self-addressed slips,
the rejections you sent
yourself. Laugh at yourself,
the little hope you had,
scratched out with "find your voice,"
or "show and don't tell," or
"your story doesn't meet
the needs of this issue."

The issue with your needs
is that I don't know what
you need, and neither do
you. Needs? You don't need this
poem, and I don't need
this nonsense anymore.

But calm down, keep working,
become an "exciting,

new voice" a "writer to watch."
Fuck. Honestly, as hard
as you work, you won't be
able to rub two cents
together with this shit.

Phonography 2.0

Matt Gold

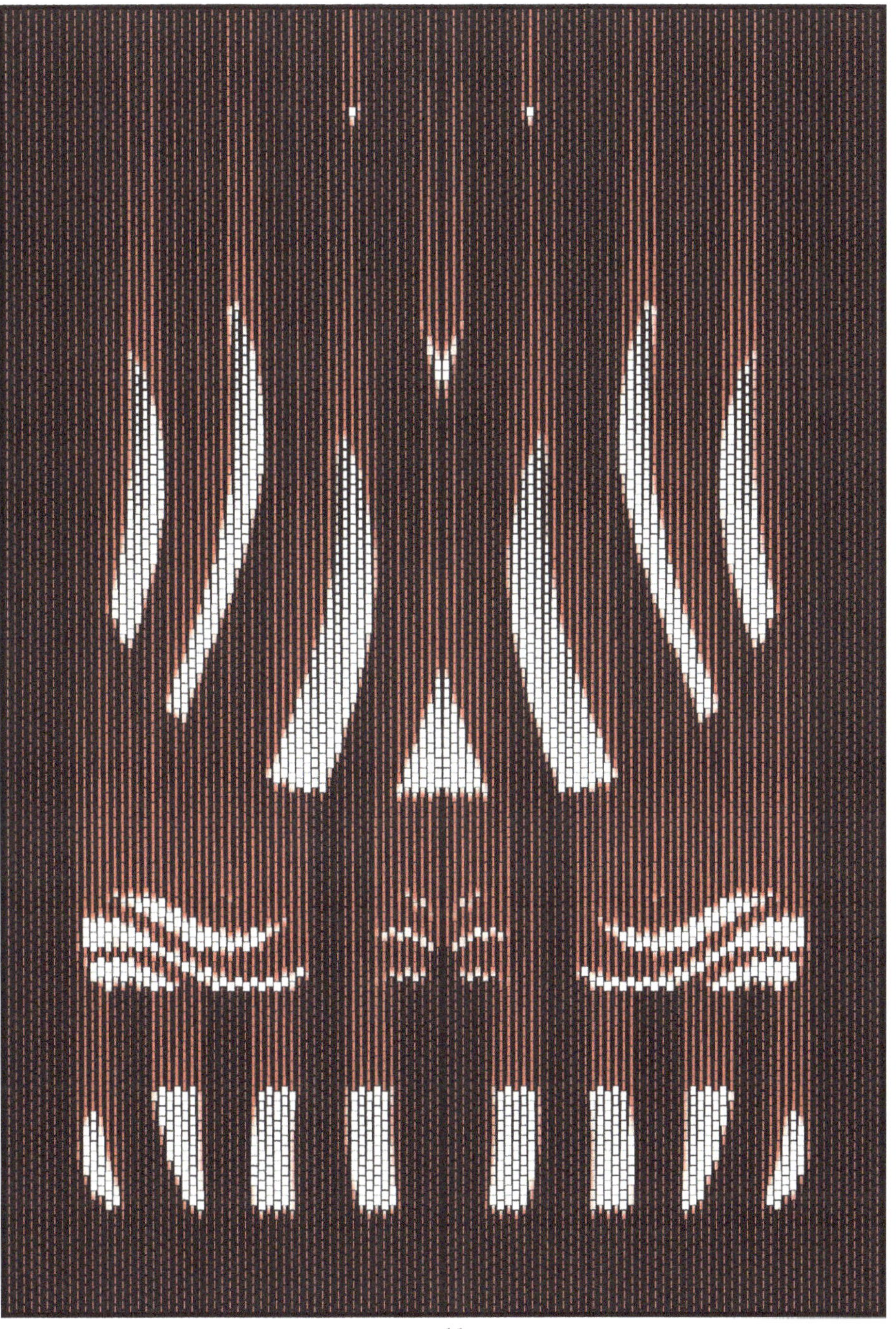

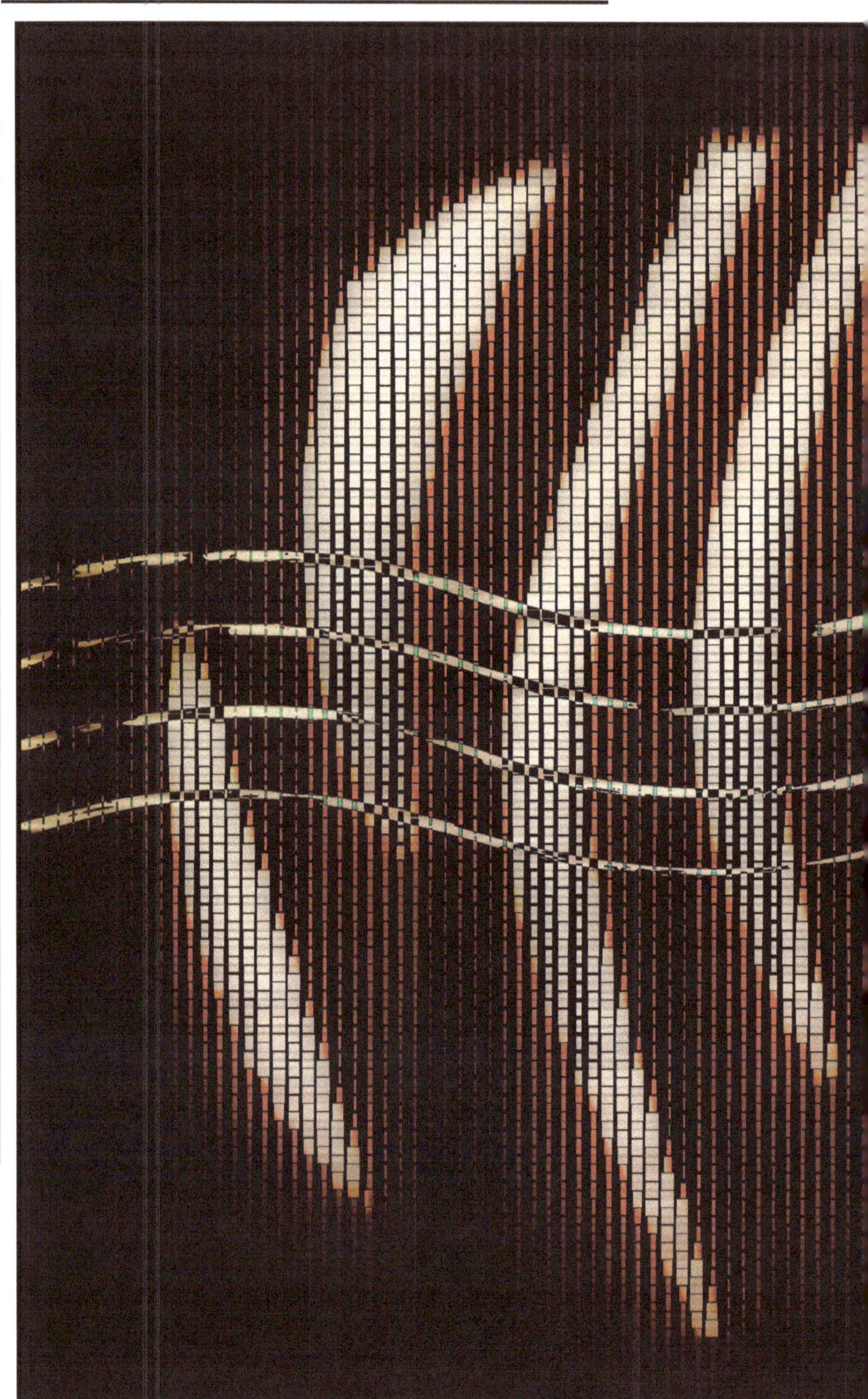

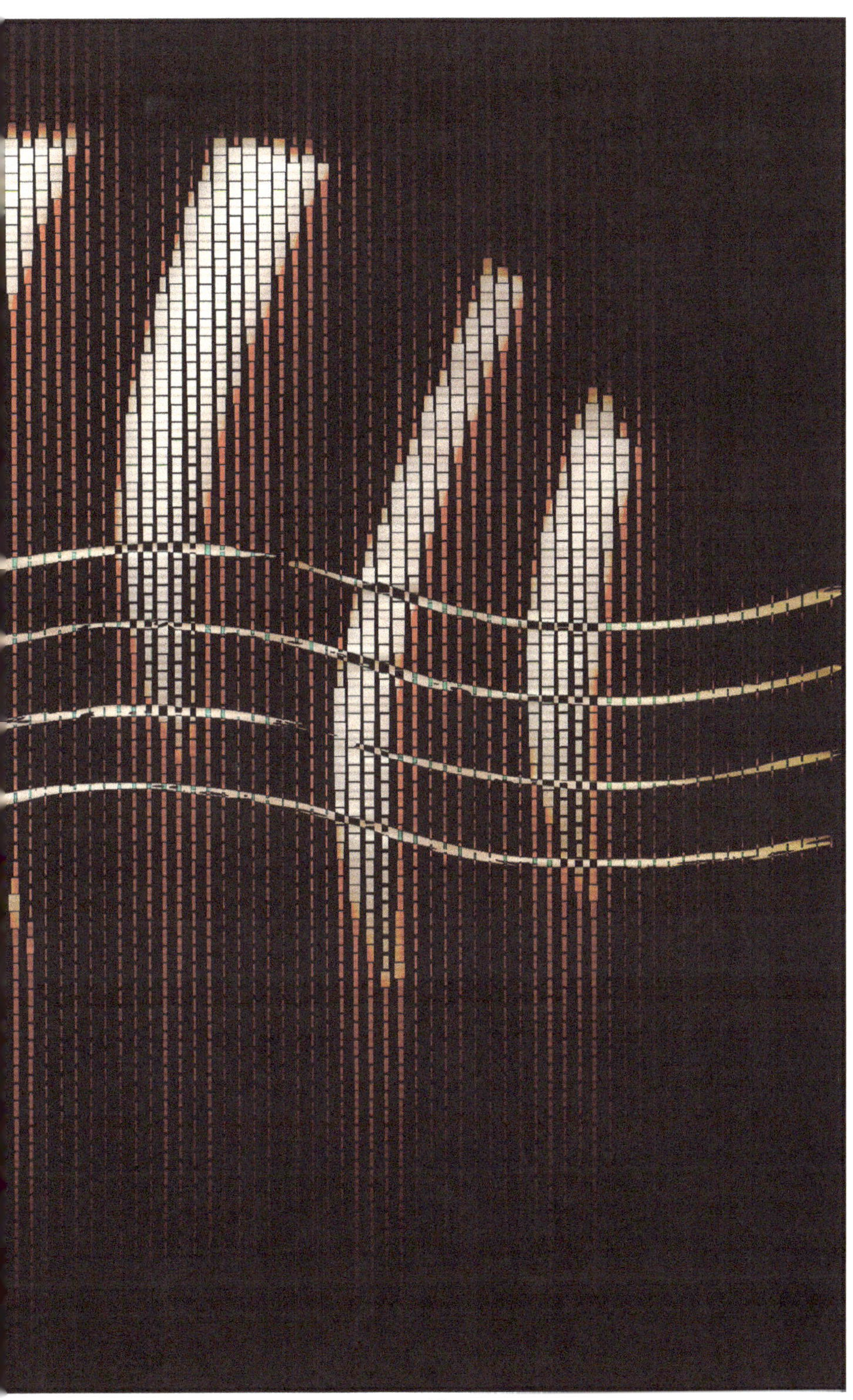

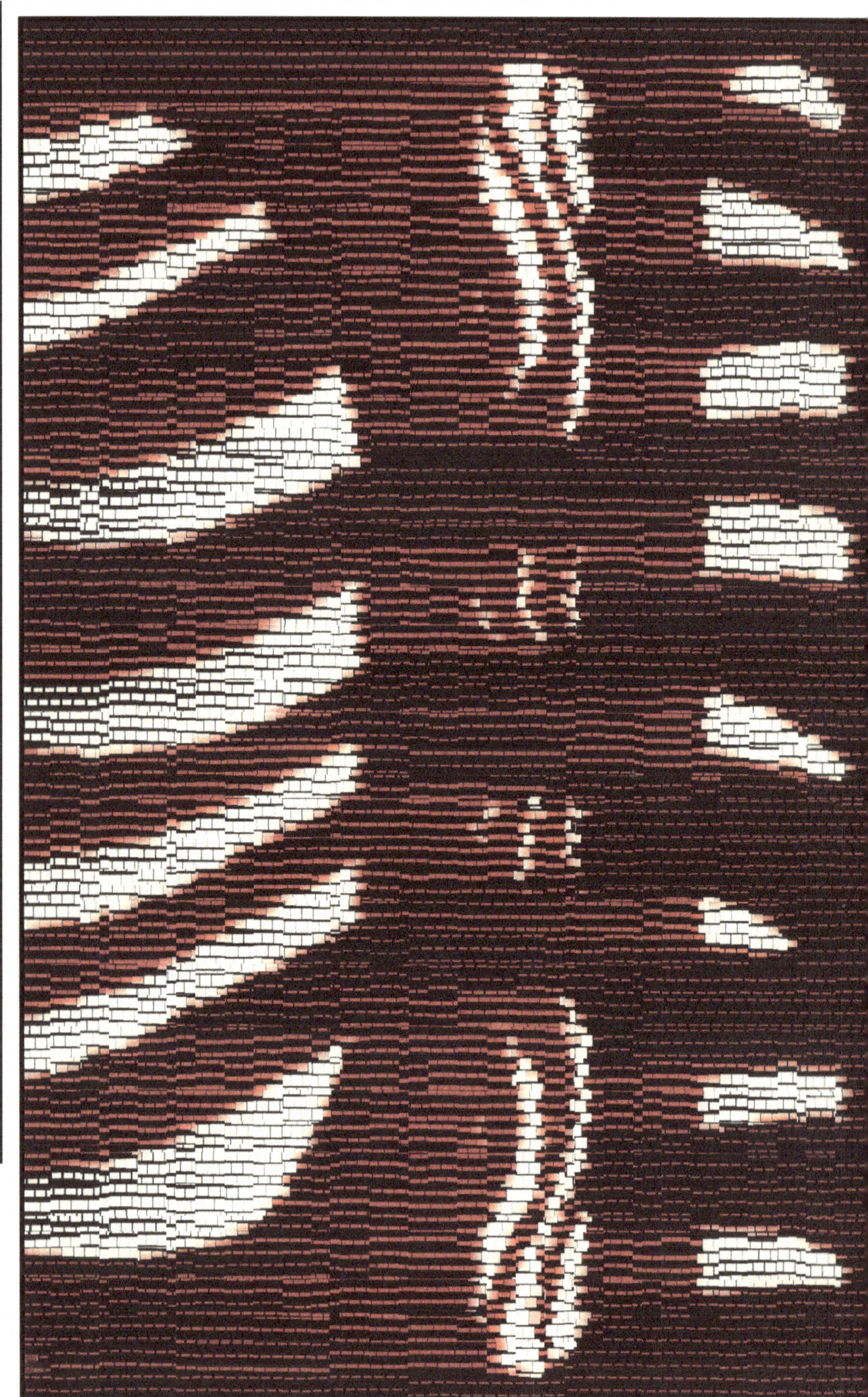

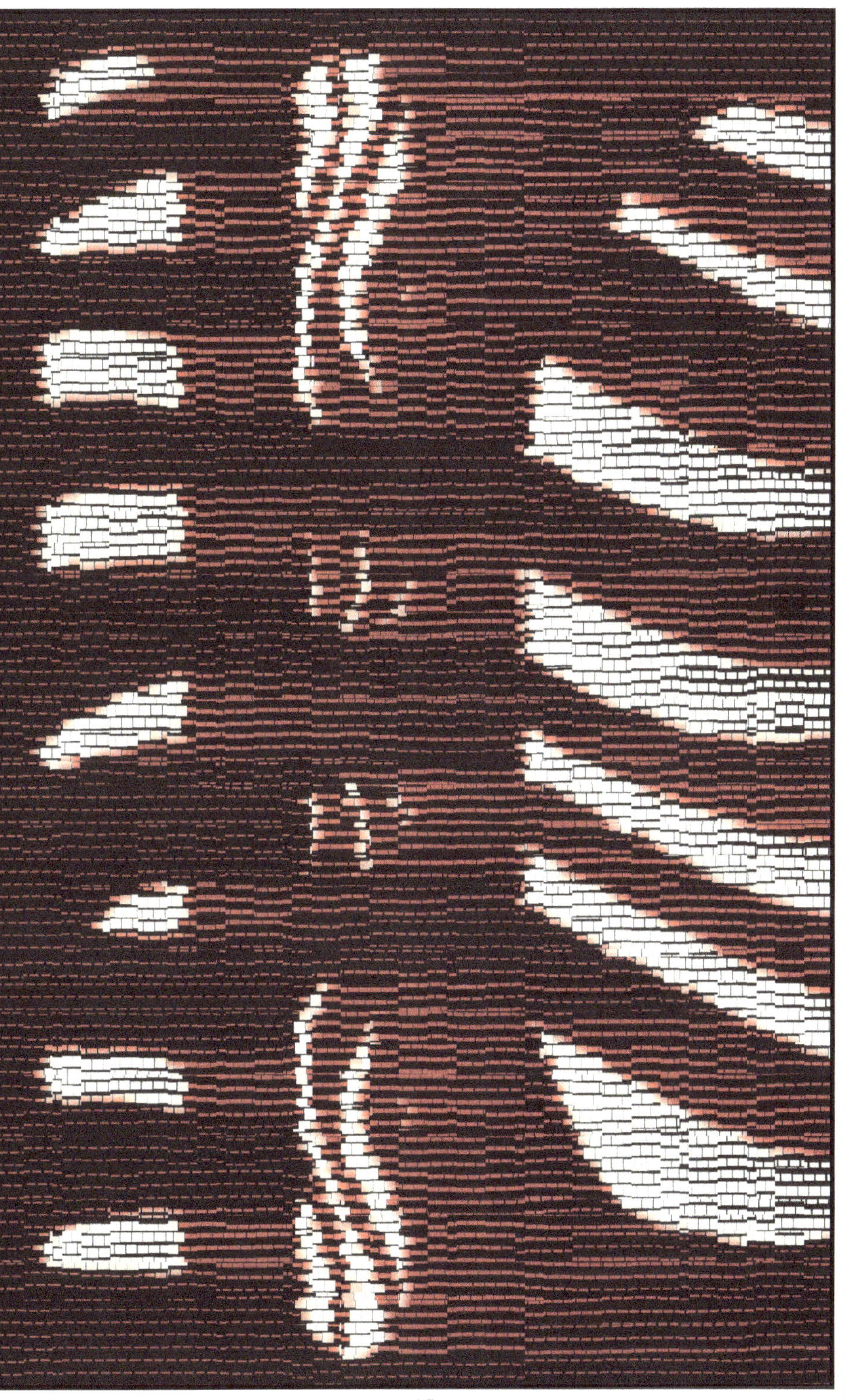

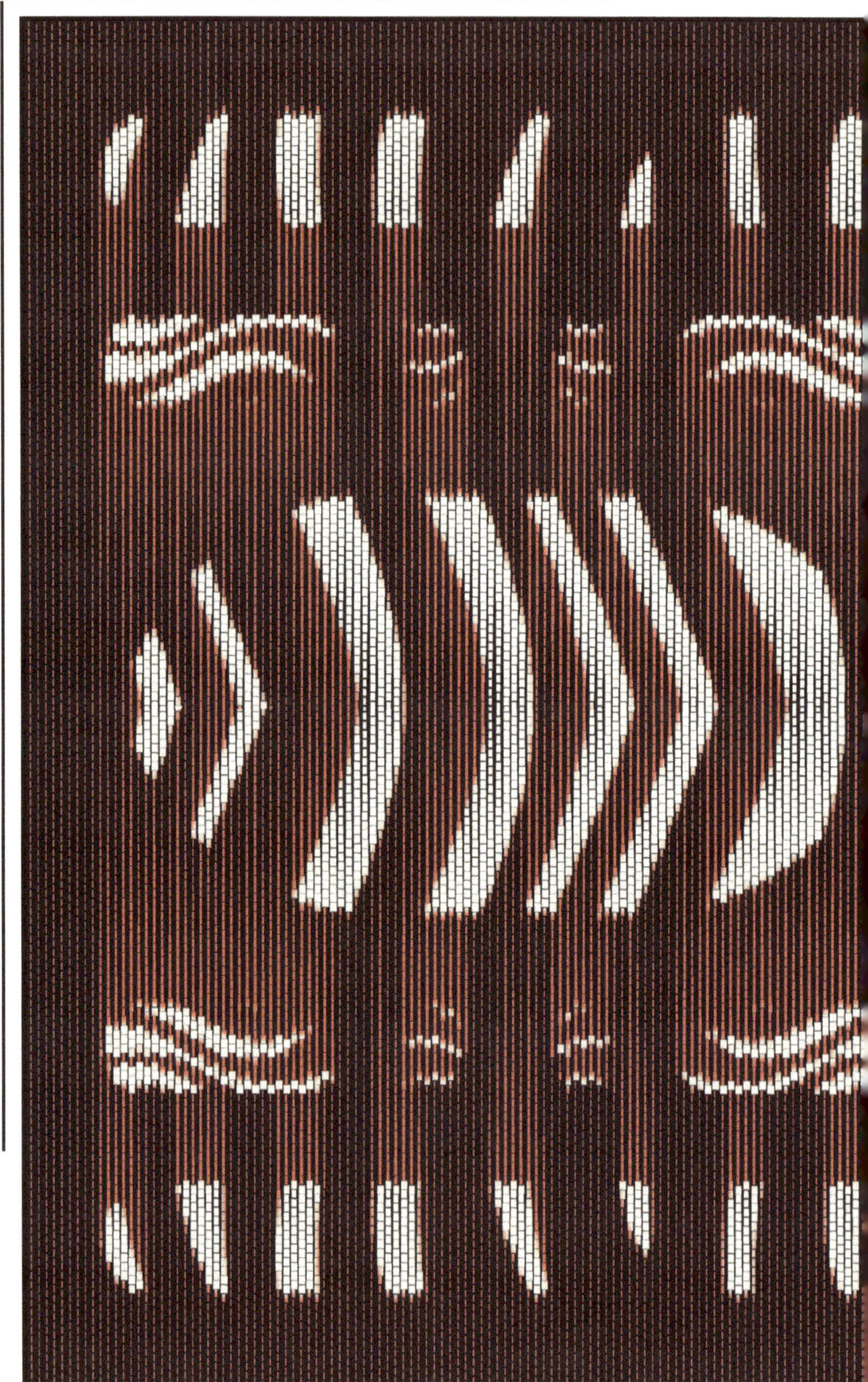

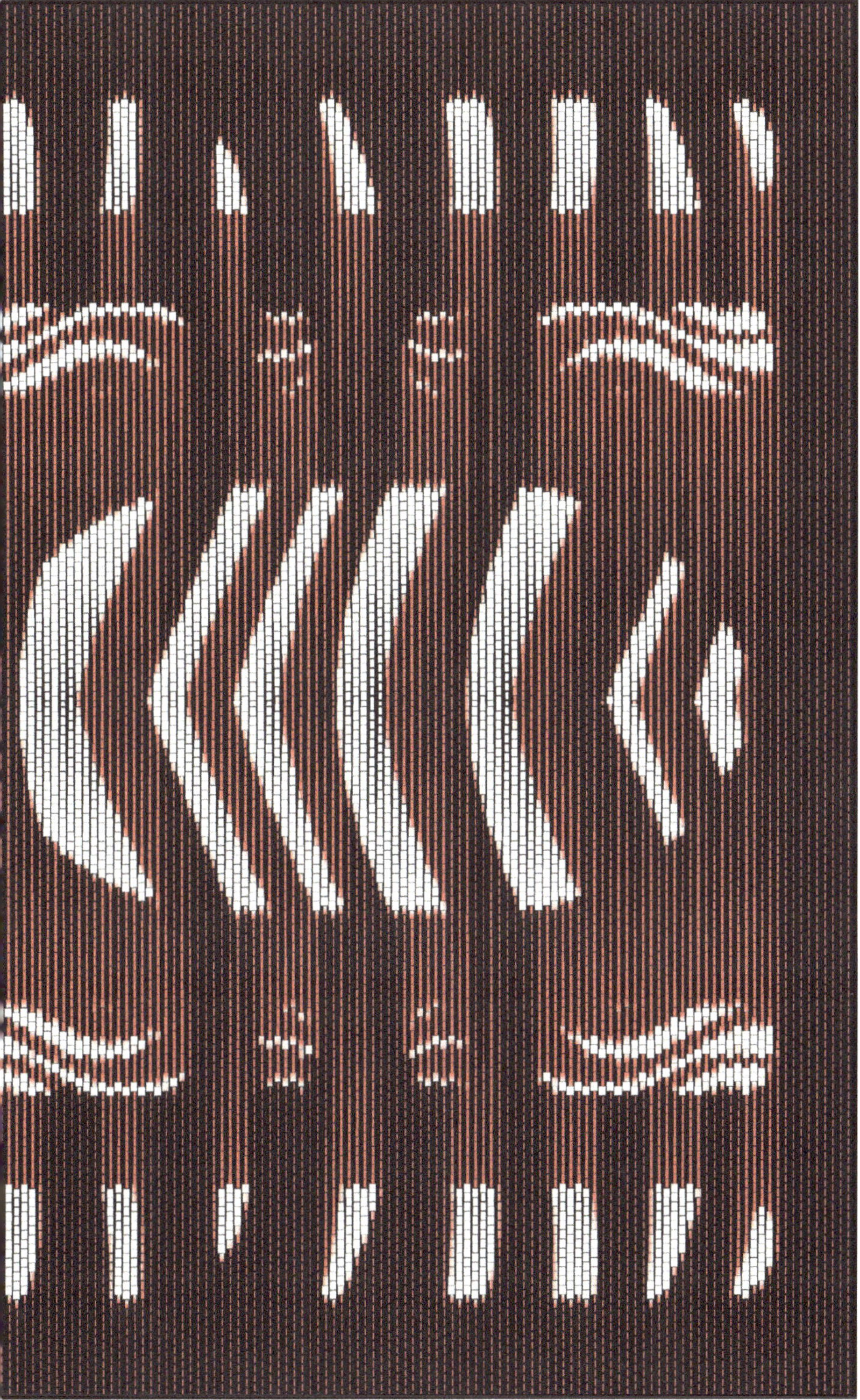

Salvador's Grave

Jeffery Lincoln

Salvador Dali's Grave
is in a town called Figueres, Spain
near the Northeast border with France

When he was a boy, Dali's father
Left him with a book showing images
of untreated venereal diseases
To educate him about sex

Dali rose to great prominence
Met Sigmund Freud
And appeared on the Dick Cavett Show
Carrying an anteater

And The Persistence of Memory
Is one of the world's great paintings
but the one with the best name is
Skull with its Lyric Appendage
Leaning on a Night Table
Which should have the Exact Temperature of a Cardinal's Bird's Nest

And Dali's Grave is in the little town where he was born
His tomb is in the middle of a museum
And it's unmarked
Surrounded by his work
And people unknowingly trod on his remains
While admiring his art
And I think that's wonderful
But not fully
Which means
I'm not ready

Brink

Adele Evershed

The corpse bird waits for the last leaf

I once could stroll home no matter the hour

Now my asking sounds like begging

And I am worse off than a widower

As your corpse is still here to remind me

I try to stretch resolve and splinter clouds

But my body is lumpy—like a badger in a bag

Instead I make lists of favorite foods

—last comfort to be served by the man in the purple waistcoat

Chilled broad bean soup—gritty walnut dumplings

And for afters— hot blackcurrant tart and pouring cream

It is what it isn't—part of a thing I know now

Like taking you to Starbucks because I didn't know your name

I remember instead when the boats delivered milk and butter

Mam making pancakes as thick as her stockings

And the skipping forecast rattling through the radio.

Sheep in the meadow, cows in the corn.....

What was the month that I was born?

Ha I'm a poet and I don't know it!

The cat layered on my lap like a gravity blanket

Her indifference has the insistence of rheumatism

I think I am a dog person—you said not

I am bothered by your smell—sweet like subterfuge

'No pissing in the alley' you shout, but I'm desperate

When falling try not to scream and disturb the robin

That death bird might take my corpse

And refashion it into a rope as round as a puddle

Am I waning? Waning after waxing. All things bright and gone

Don't grieve—you can't weep for someone you never knew

Tell it all to the paper doves or the last poppies

Petals like eyelids, seeds like black holes—gone in a blink

I wonder—am I going to heaven or hell or to the Vegan Kitchen?

I think I eat bacon—a woman called Ruth says not

As she spoons bile between my lips or maybe it's just jello

Facing It Together

Jack Bordnick

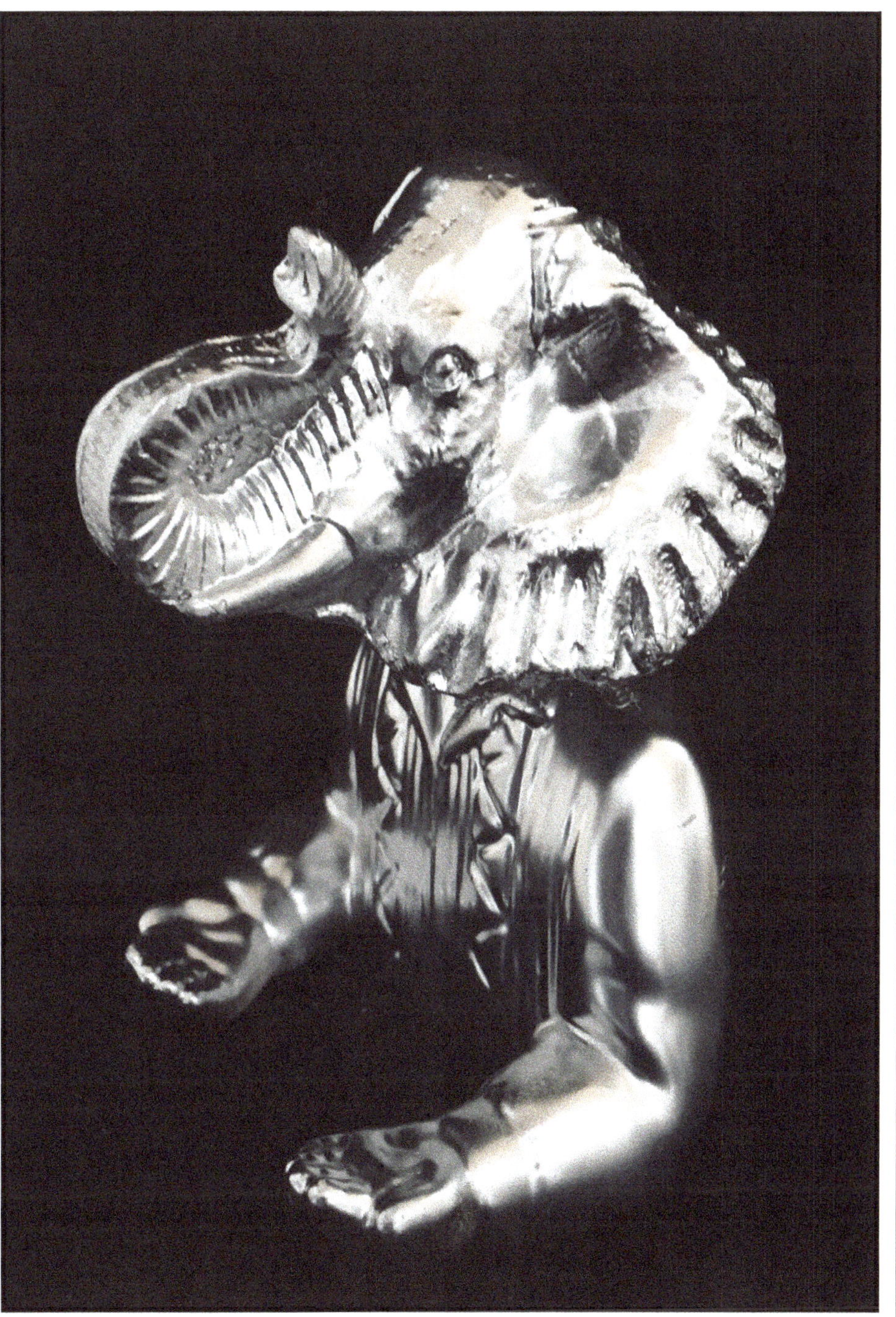

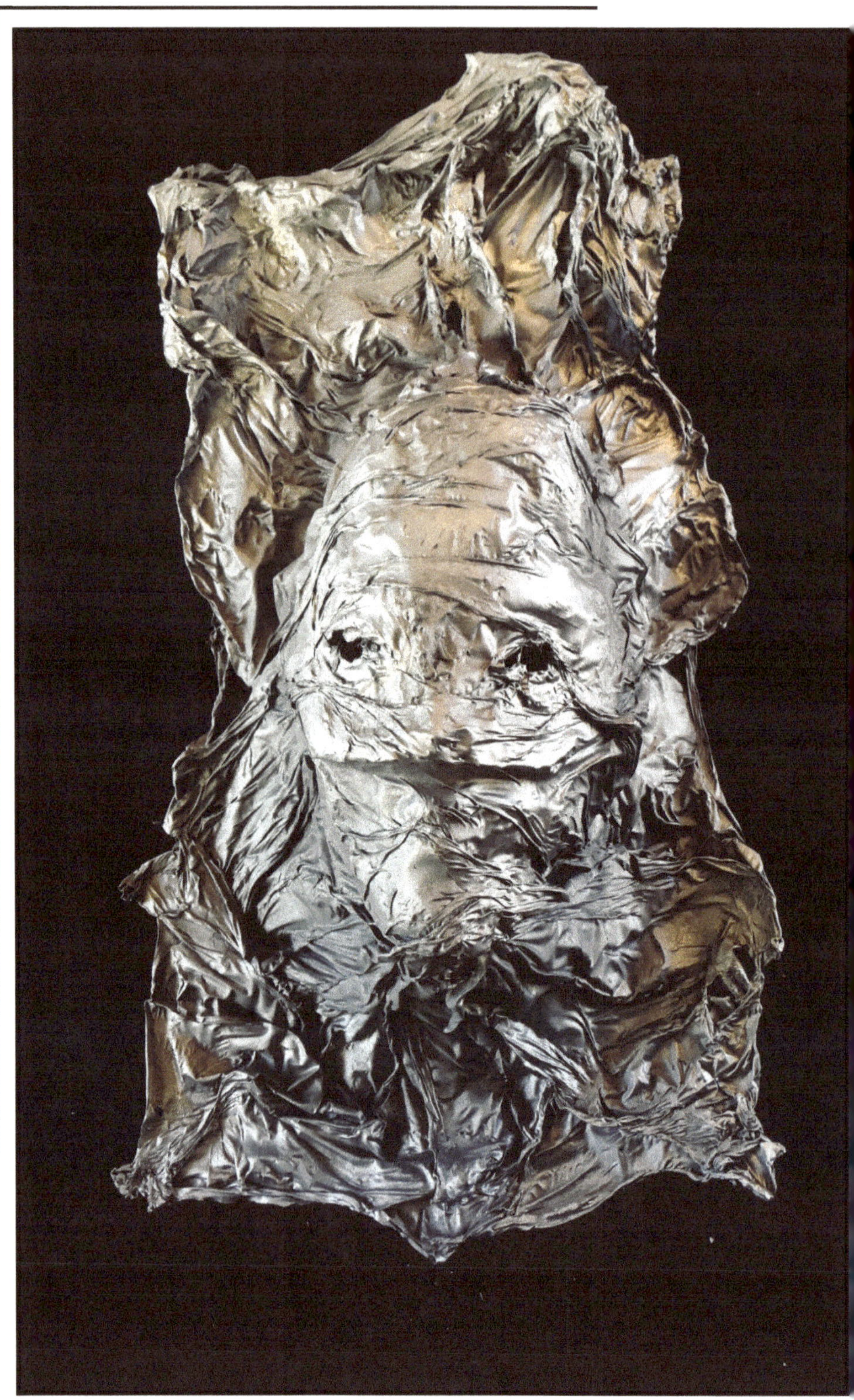

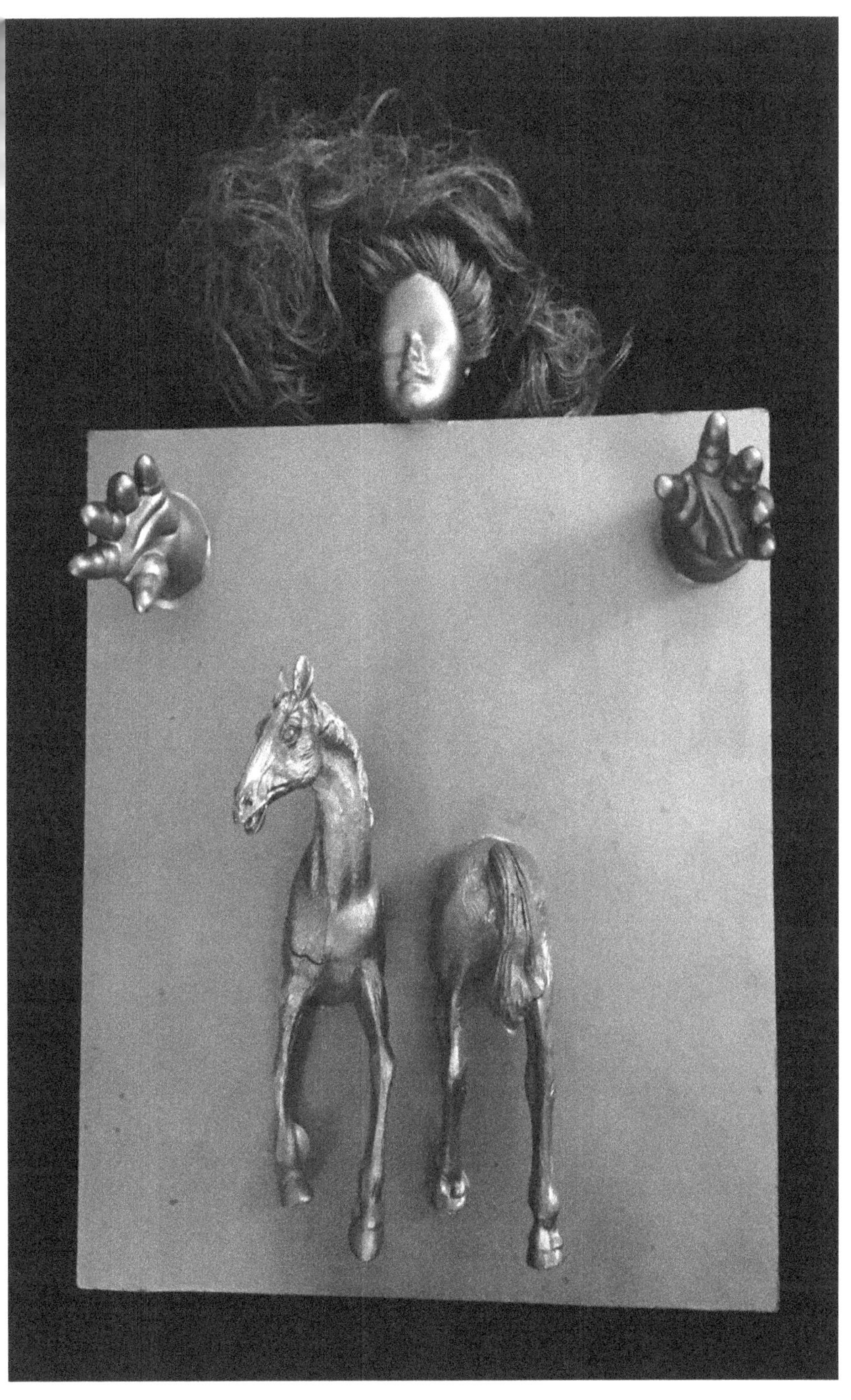

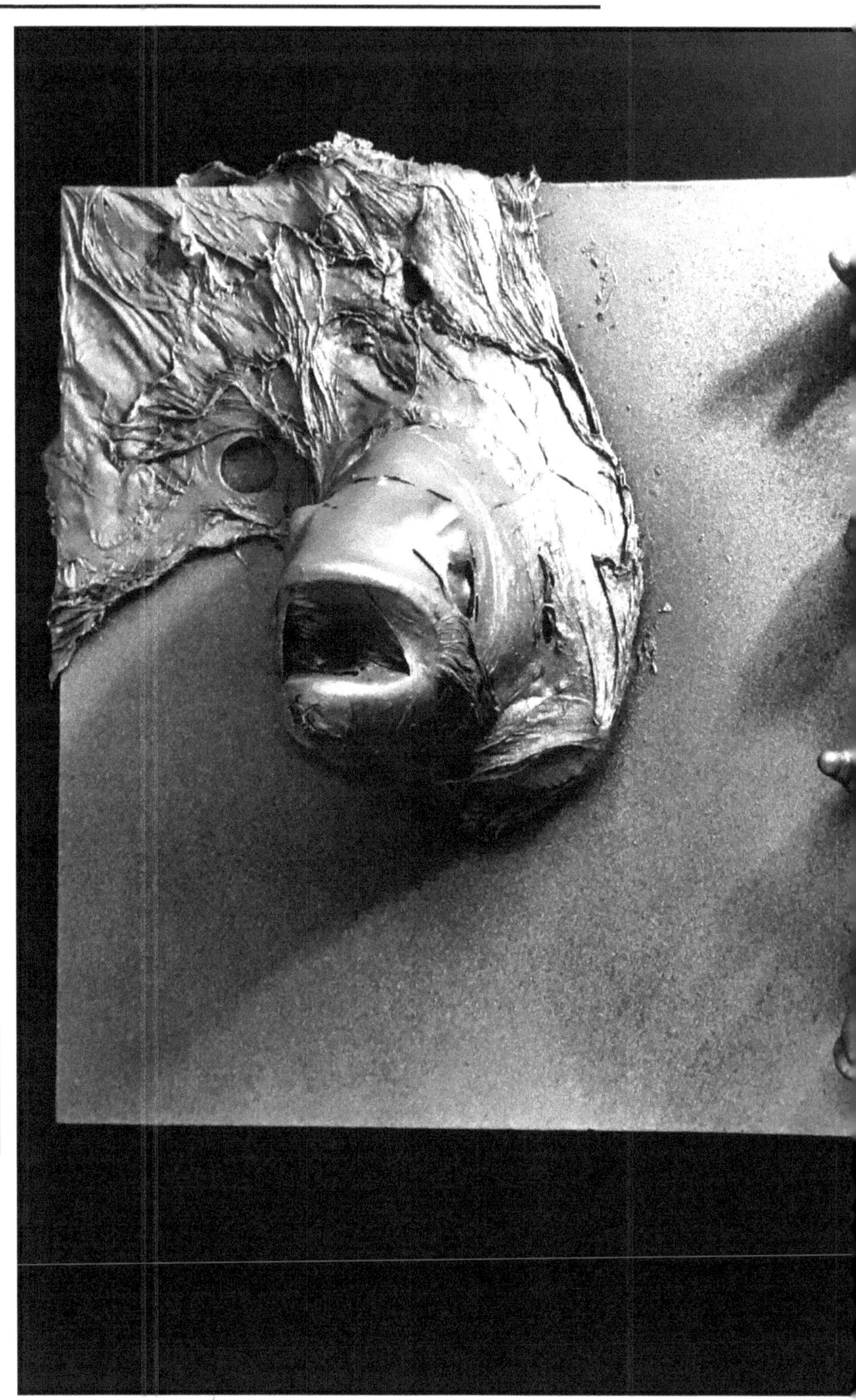

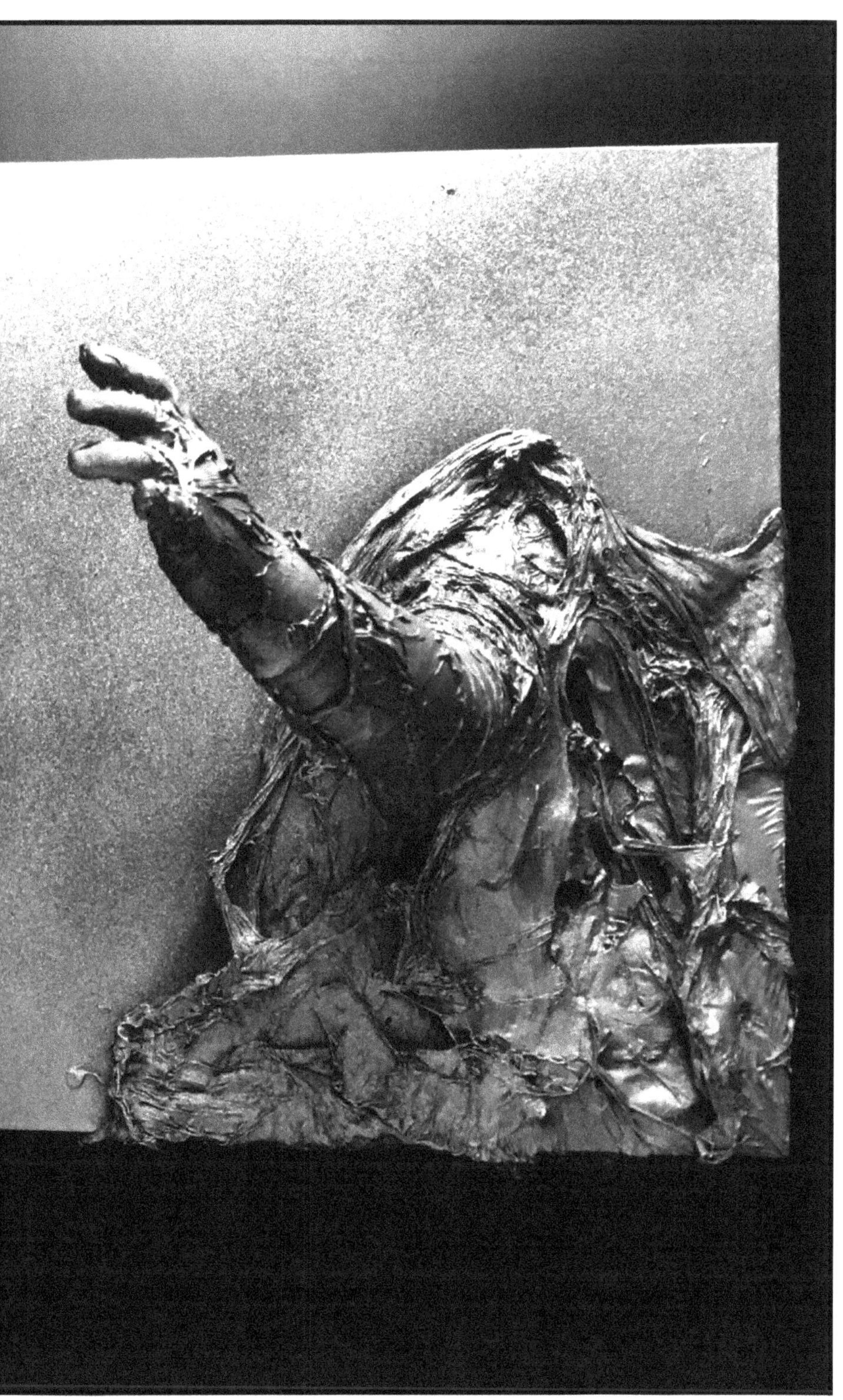

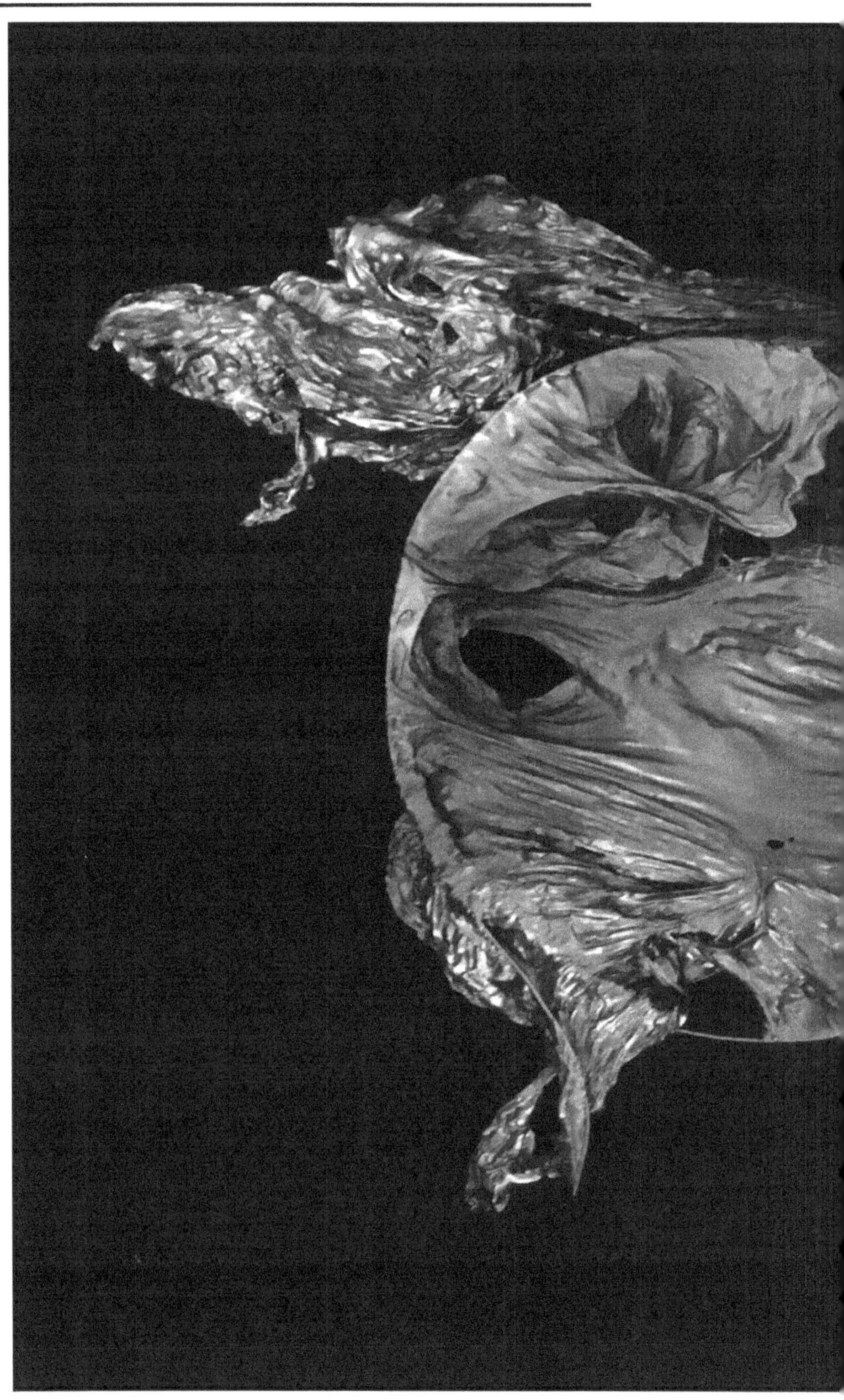

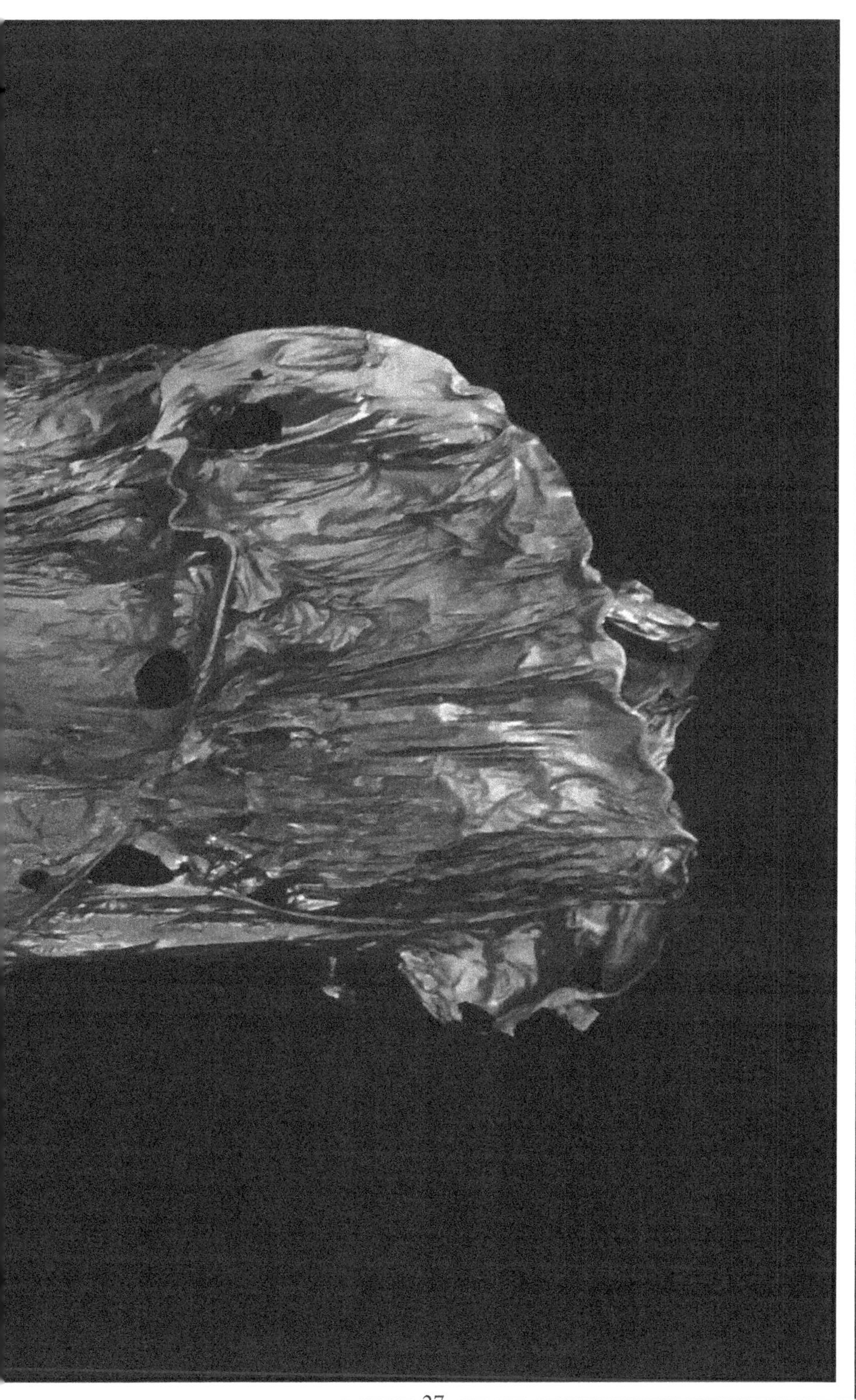

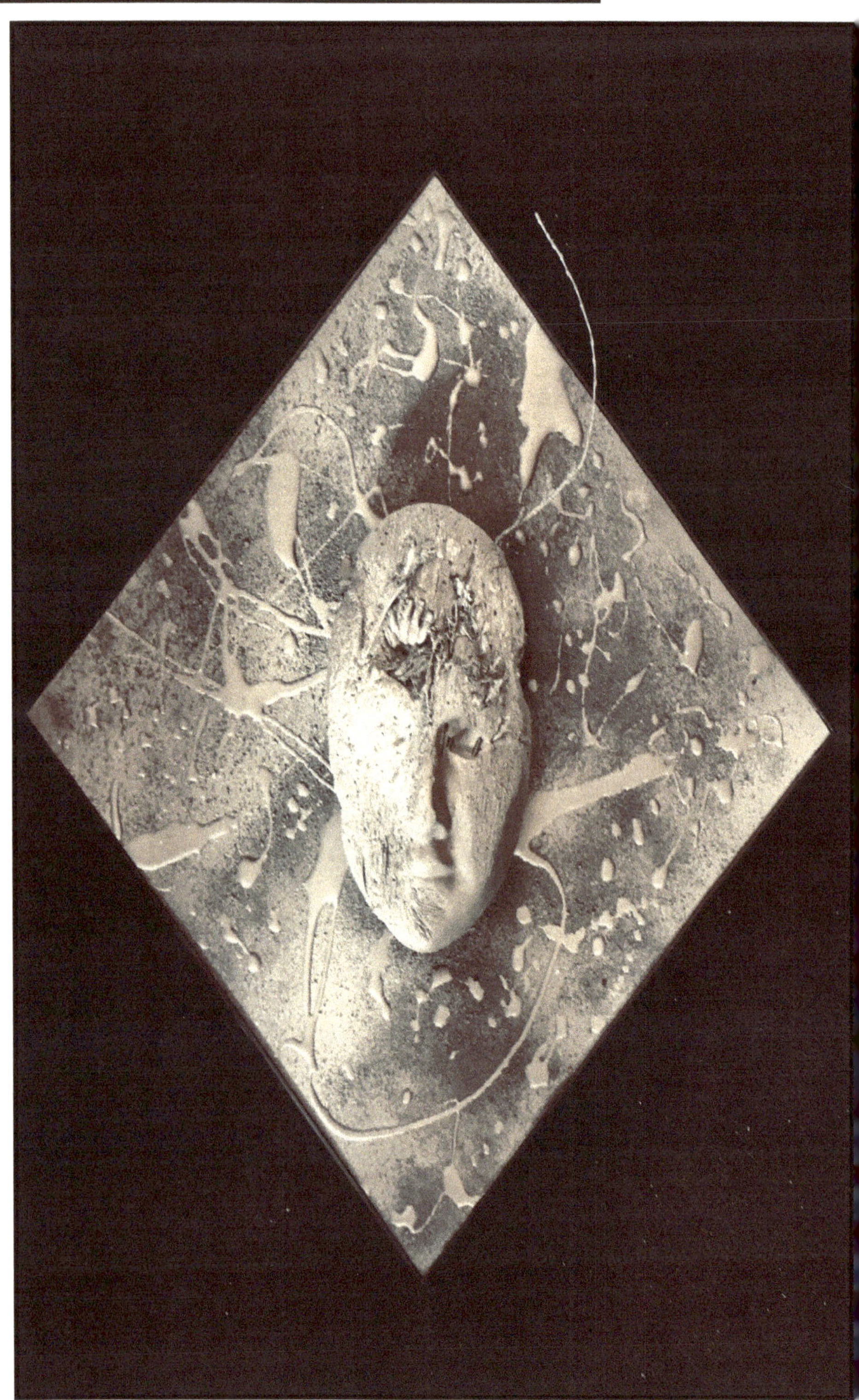

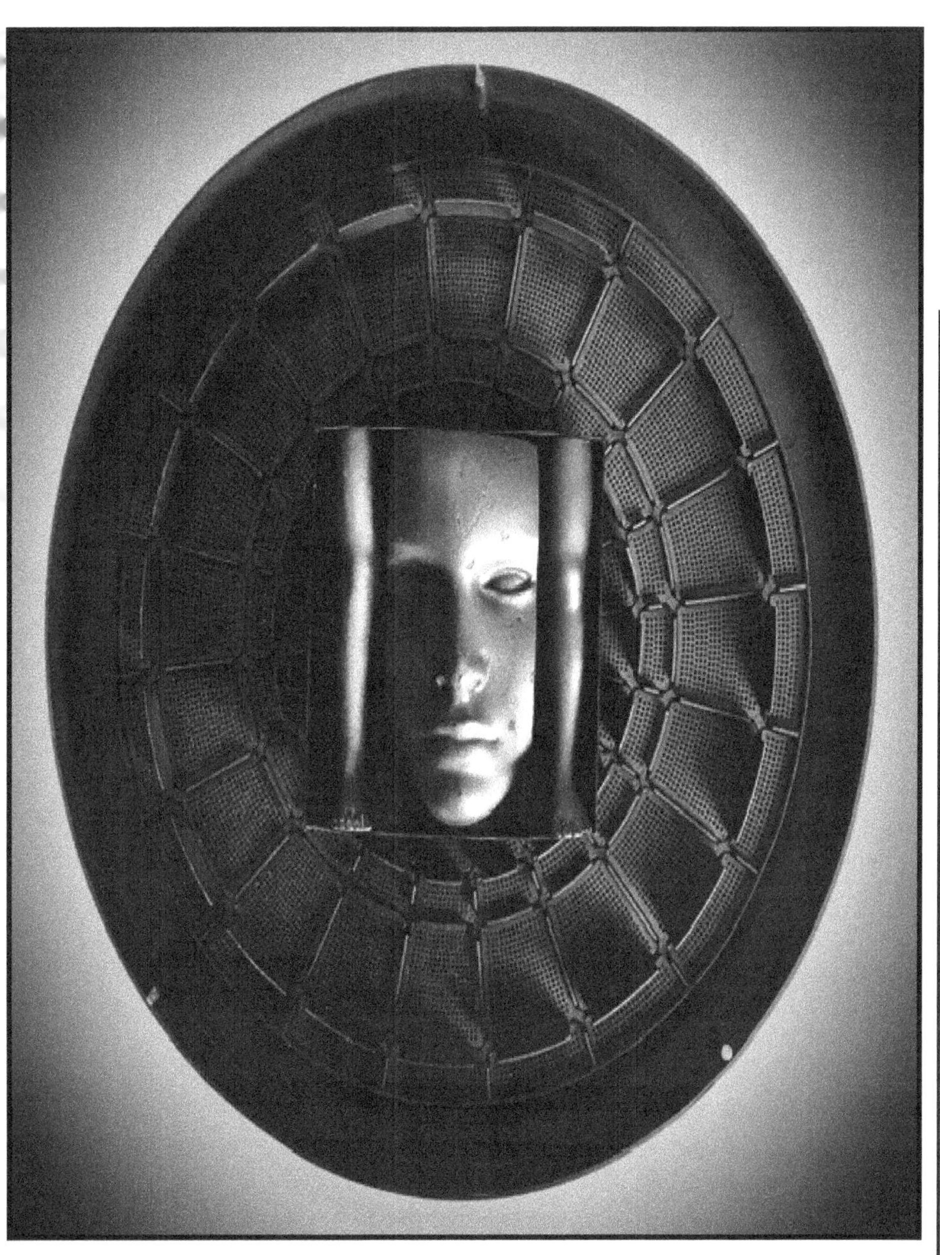

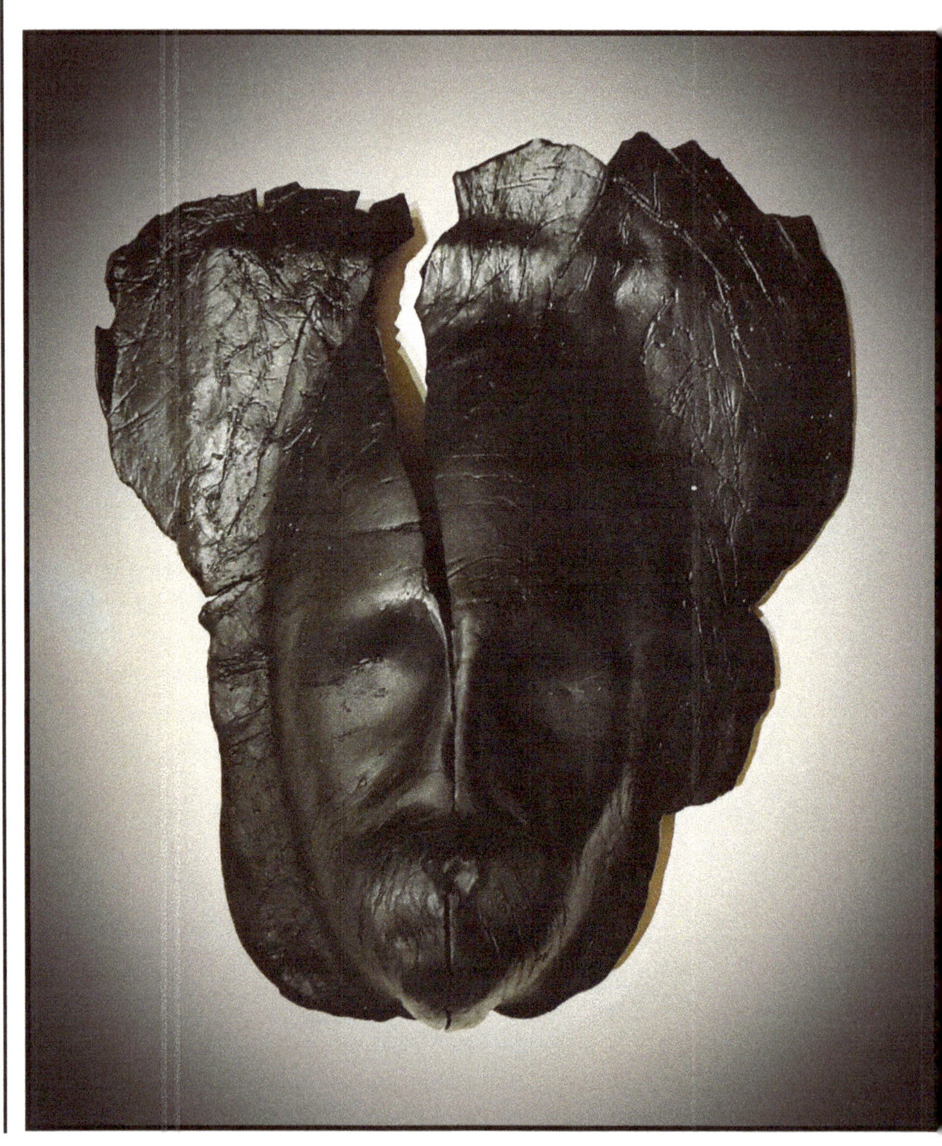

Exhibition

Marco Buttice

You are here
About five feet before me
But I cannot touch your artistry,
They simply won't allow it.
The velour rope separates us,
But our archive binds us.

I imagine what would happen
If I crossed that line,
Caressing your frame
Into my willing arms.
Maybe I'd turn into marble,
Or bleed out like watercolour.

I'll be your beholder
Singing like a church choir,
Devilish and delicious.
The bodies swarm us,
But it's not pictures they want.

Turning My Things Into Garbage

Heather Gluck

It all has to go
I look around and realize
the vase I bought five years
ago does not work
in the room
the skirt I got last week
is not flattering so
things grow in piles
everywhere crowd my
windows burst
through my drawers
twelve tubes of mascara
bacteria-filled, they say
I dump them all out
and I throw them away
like lacing a corset I
put things in place
like bleaching my hair I
strip silky coat
leave rough inside
exposed
I imagine a suburban home
where I pull weeds wildly
leave the lawn in
empty order
where new flowers sprout
and protest
my vanity stupidity
but unlike weeds that
reanimate the wasteland
I bring chaos back
I buy the stuff that swells
in the corners on the chairs
its value lost
on me today
the joy of getting melts
the misery of having
like Edie and her mother
among stacks of old records
afghans newspapers
cans for raccoons

hardly noticed the fleas
over her singing
danced the
Charleston for the camera
and kicked aside the
rotting food, made a stage
of buckling floorboards
while in the distance
the sycamore shed its
gray bark and I also peeled away
the parts of me I thought I needed
with my room a mess
of half-garbage I lean myself
over my guitar and press
my finger pads
against steel that
bites back
and I will
into existence
a sense of music I
call creation and will try
not to waste it

Ma-Da-Me

Marla McFadin

Longing, leaf and caterpillar
Away from the salted wind
Heavy in my breath,
Below the tadpoles' cattails
A green slurry where
I crawl and rock and sway
From the hips, submerged,
pending across the far-Then,
Down into deep stone-water swirl,
Aching. My small dimpled knuckles
Grab and rap bones
Of Before-Ones I'd found
Piled on the pond bank.

Clack-a-mama, come for me!
Stay for me.
Rise up through the grey clouds'
Weighted present. Now!
Hollow out, whistle and hum.
Charm glad teeth from my sullen lips.
Lower my cheek
To the surface of the world.
Grunt and moan with me.
Listen!
Listen into your opening
for the thrumming canticle of Old-new.

Am I crying?
		Or am I crying out?

Dreaming mushroom, lichen and moth,
Away from cool sand and dark flume
Rushing through my mind,
Come back for my little body.
Pick me up from this deserted transition.
Carry me over the cracking loam
In your daddy-arms.
Spread your fingers, big around me.
Bear my dangling limbs back to
Our verdant home-world.
Lay me down in this

Moist corporeal peril,
Asleep now...

At last, no longer gone.

Man Down

Joanna Baxter

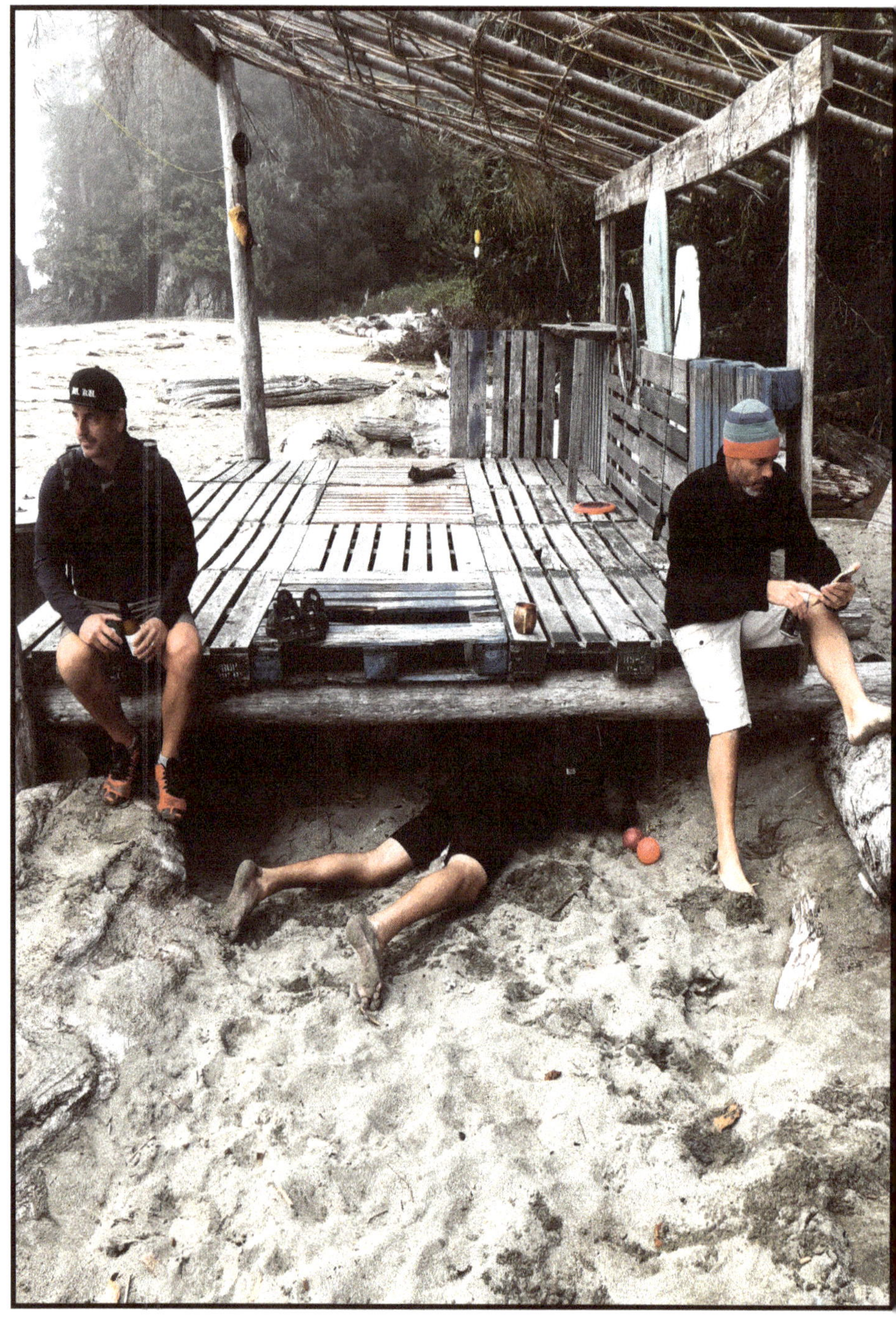

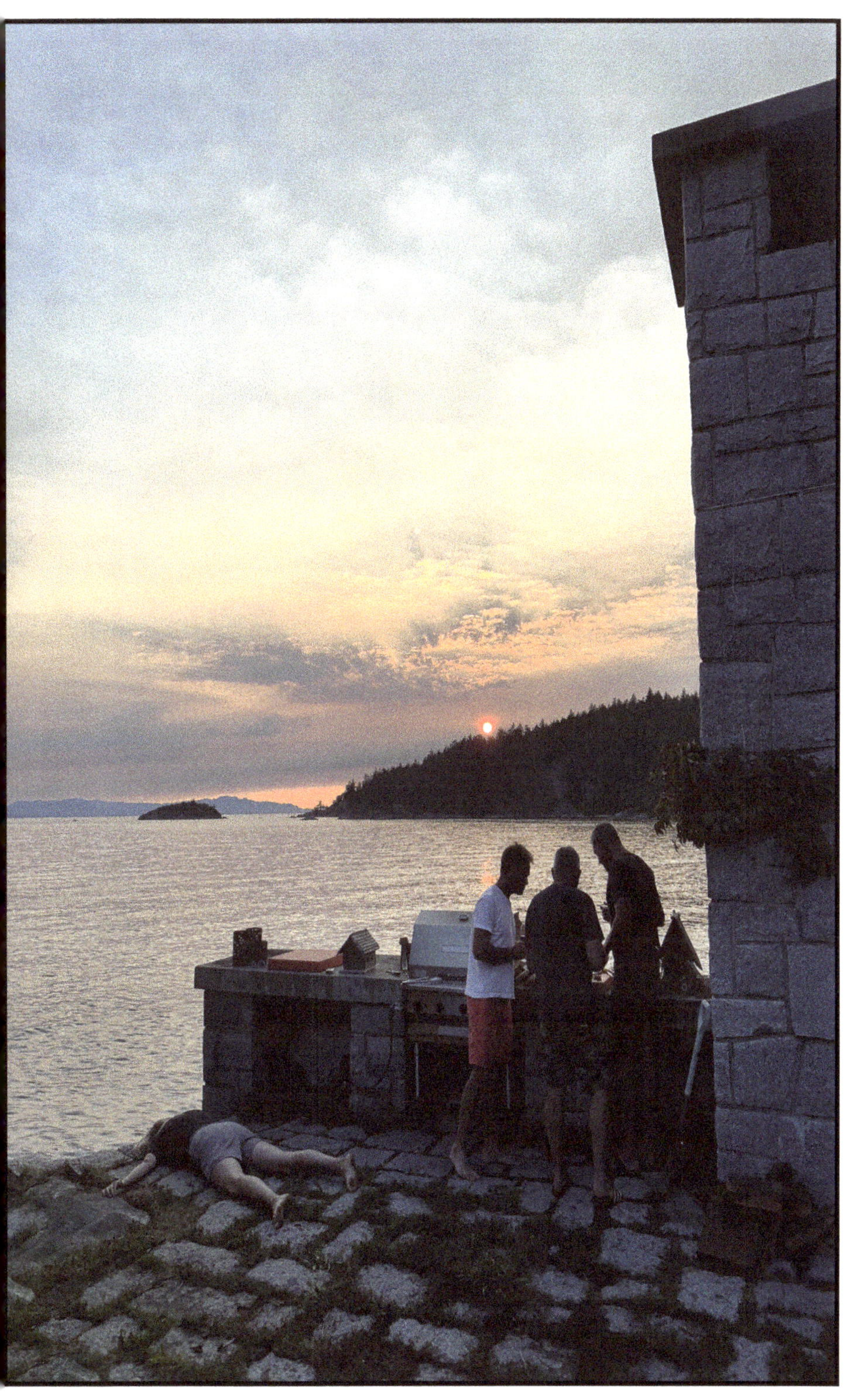

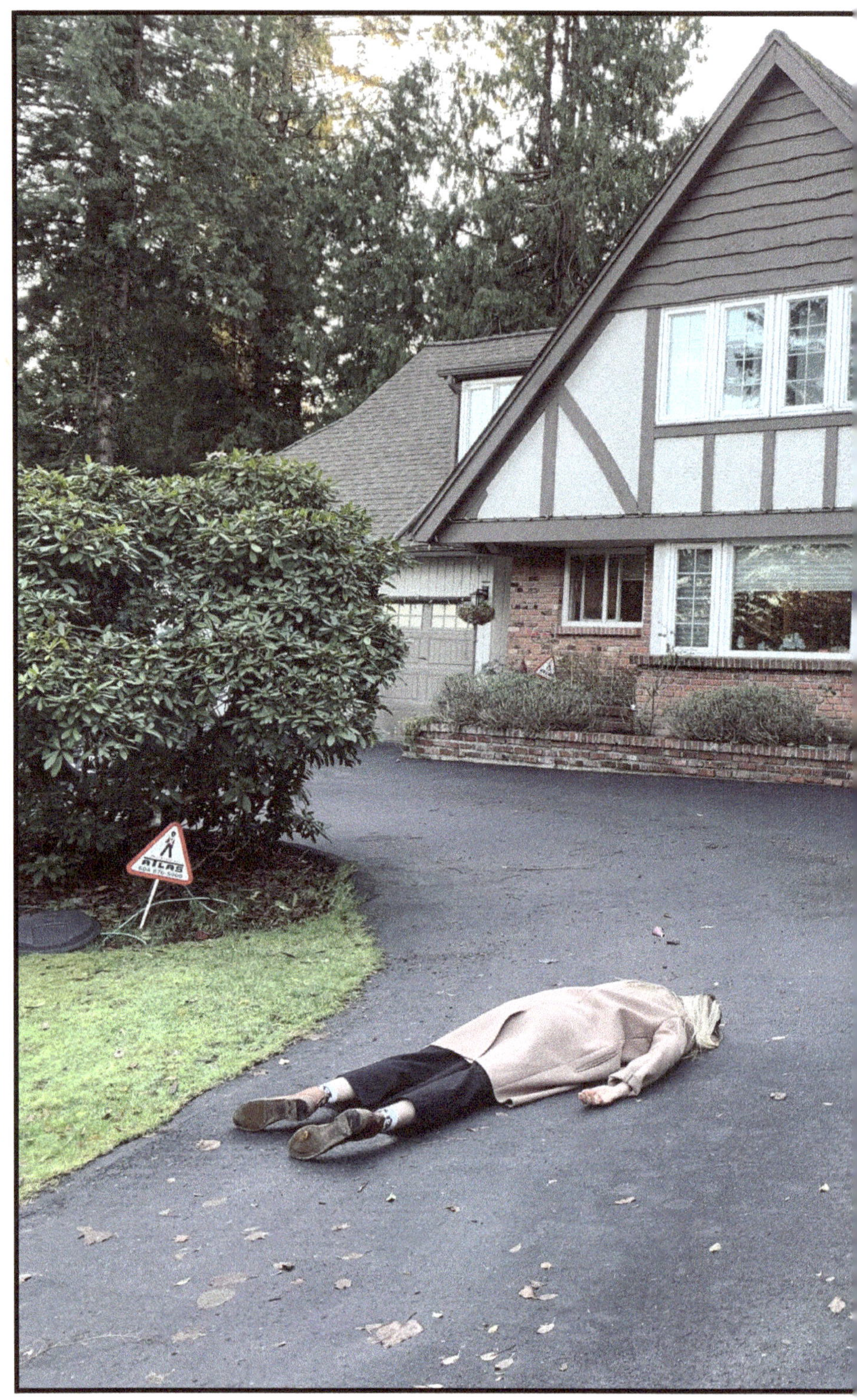

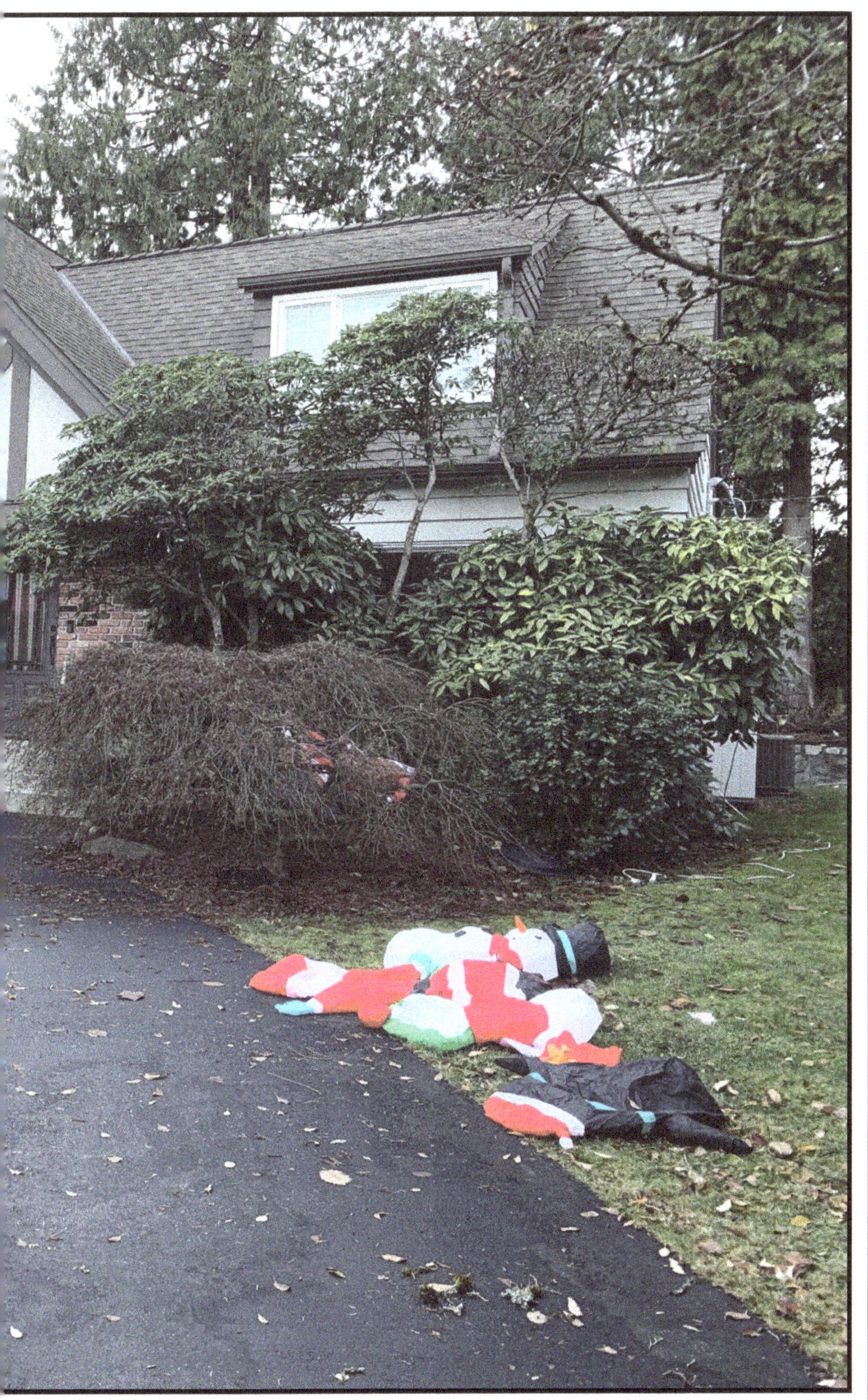

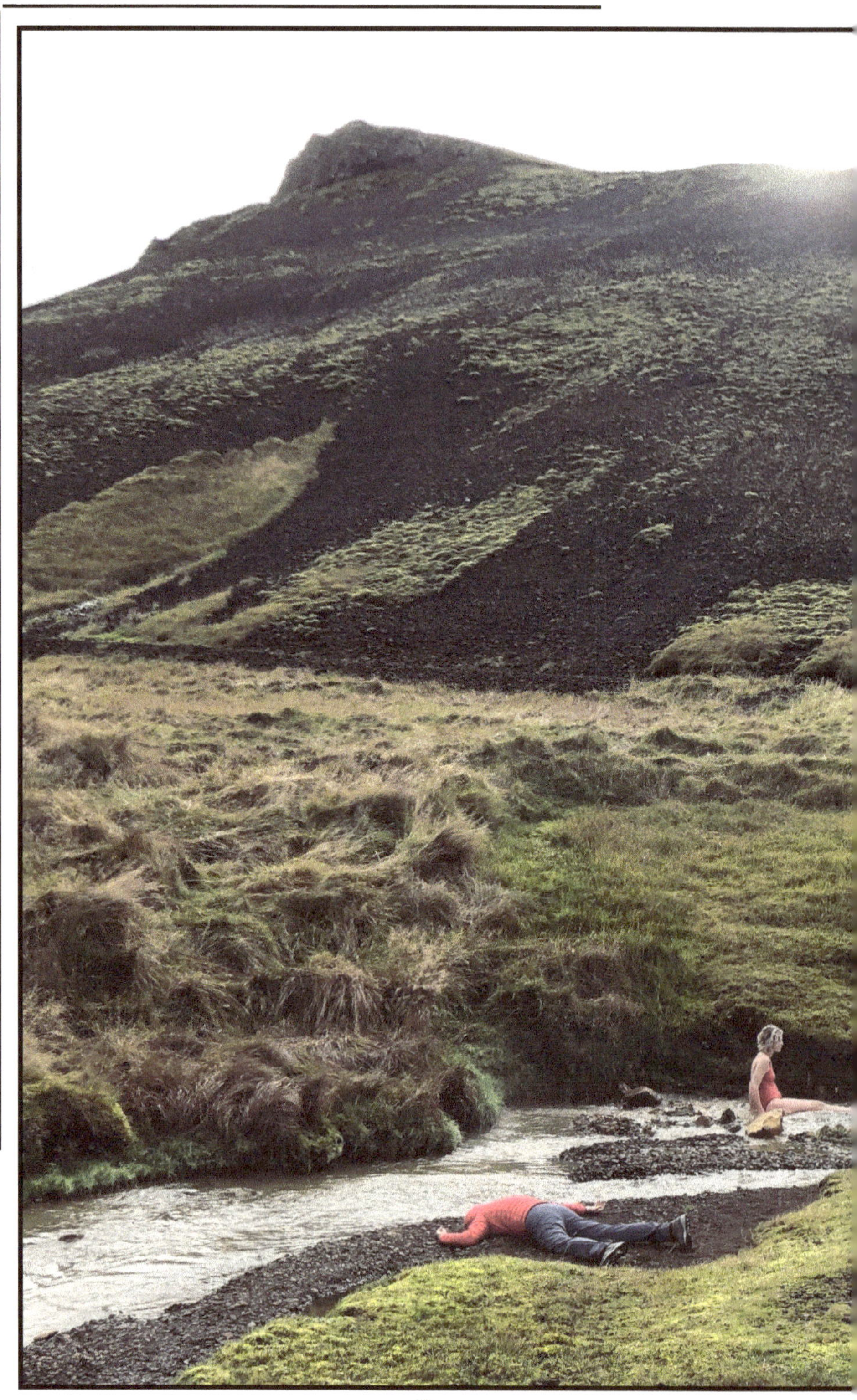

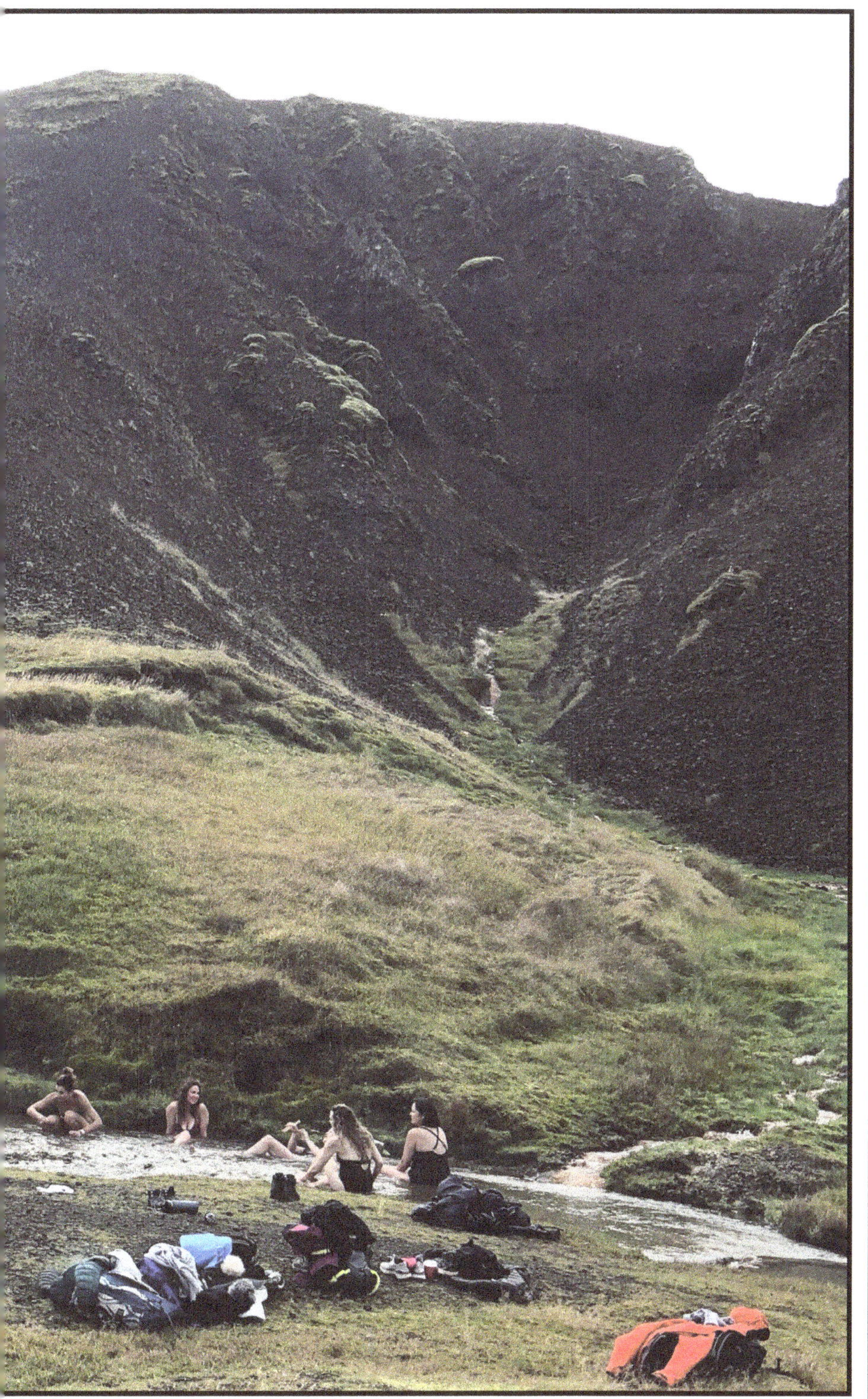

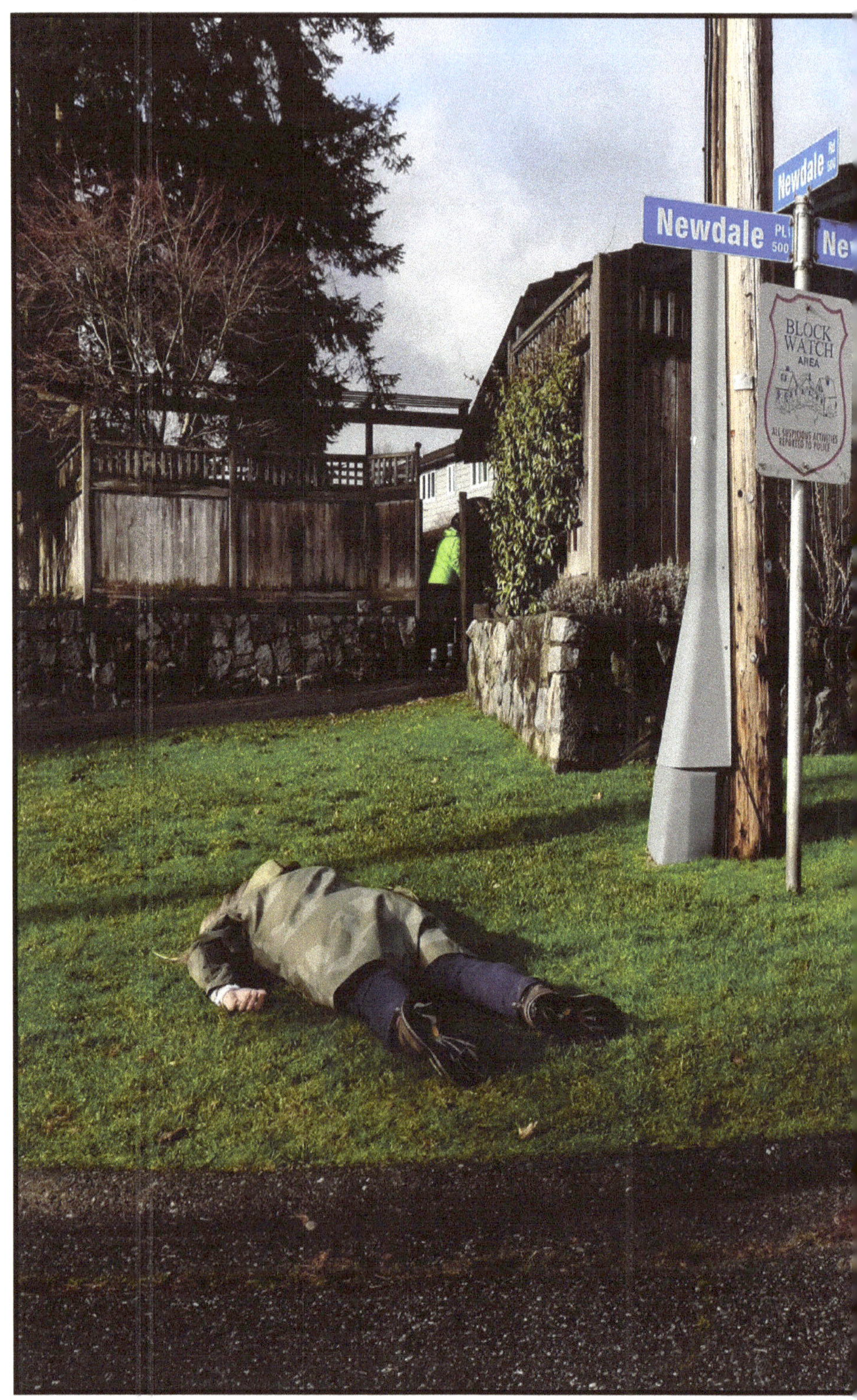

Newdale Rd 500
Newdale Pl 500
Ne
BLOCK WATCH AREA
ALL SUSPICIOUS ACTIVITIES REPORTED TO POLICE

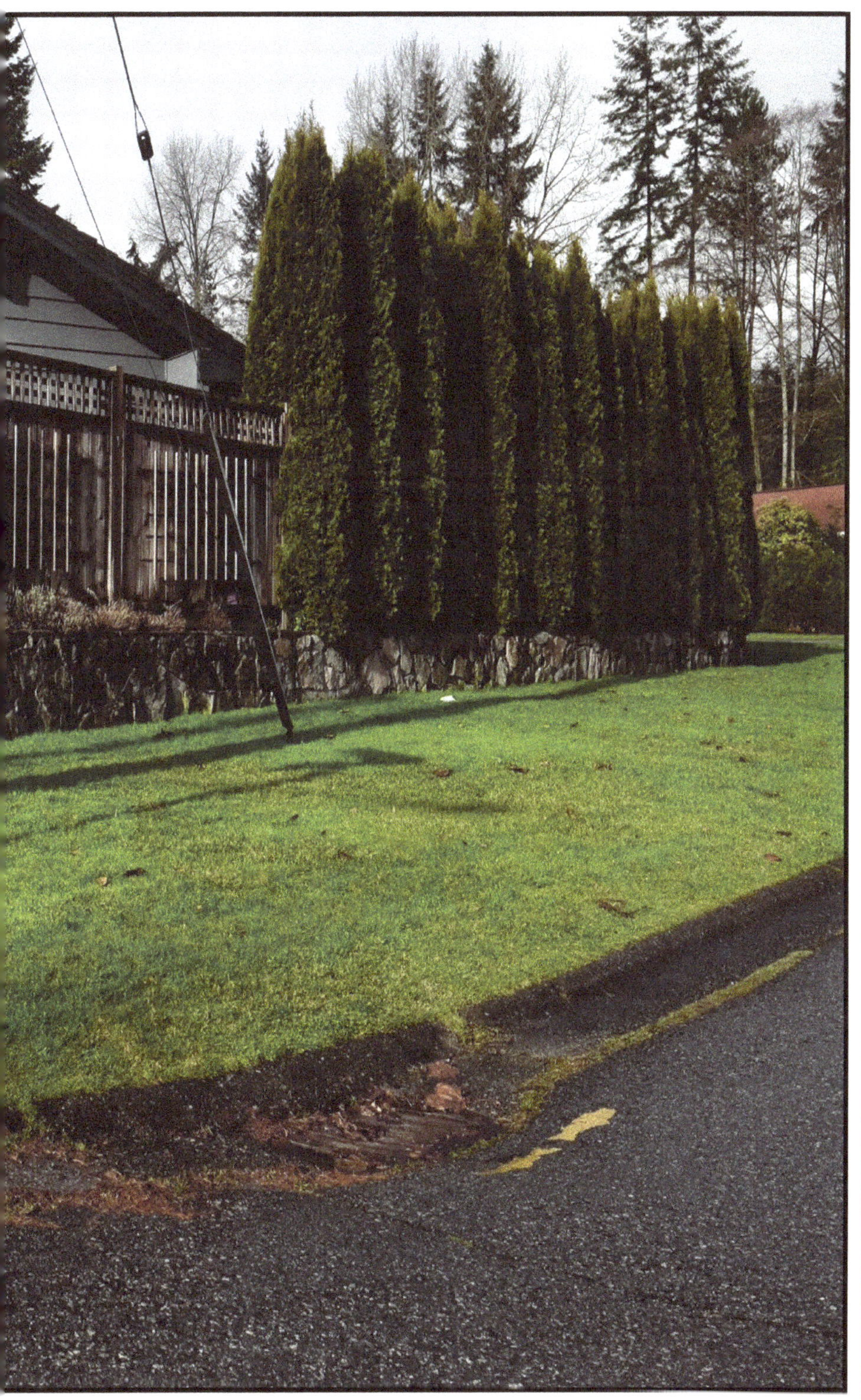

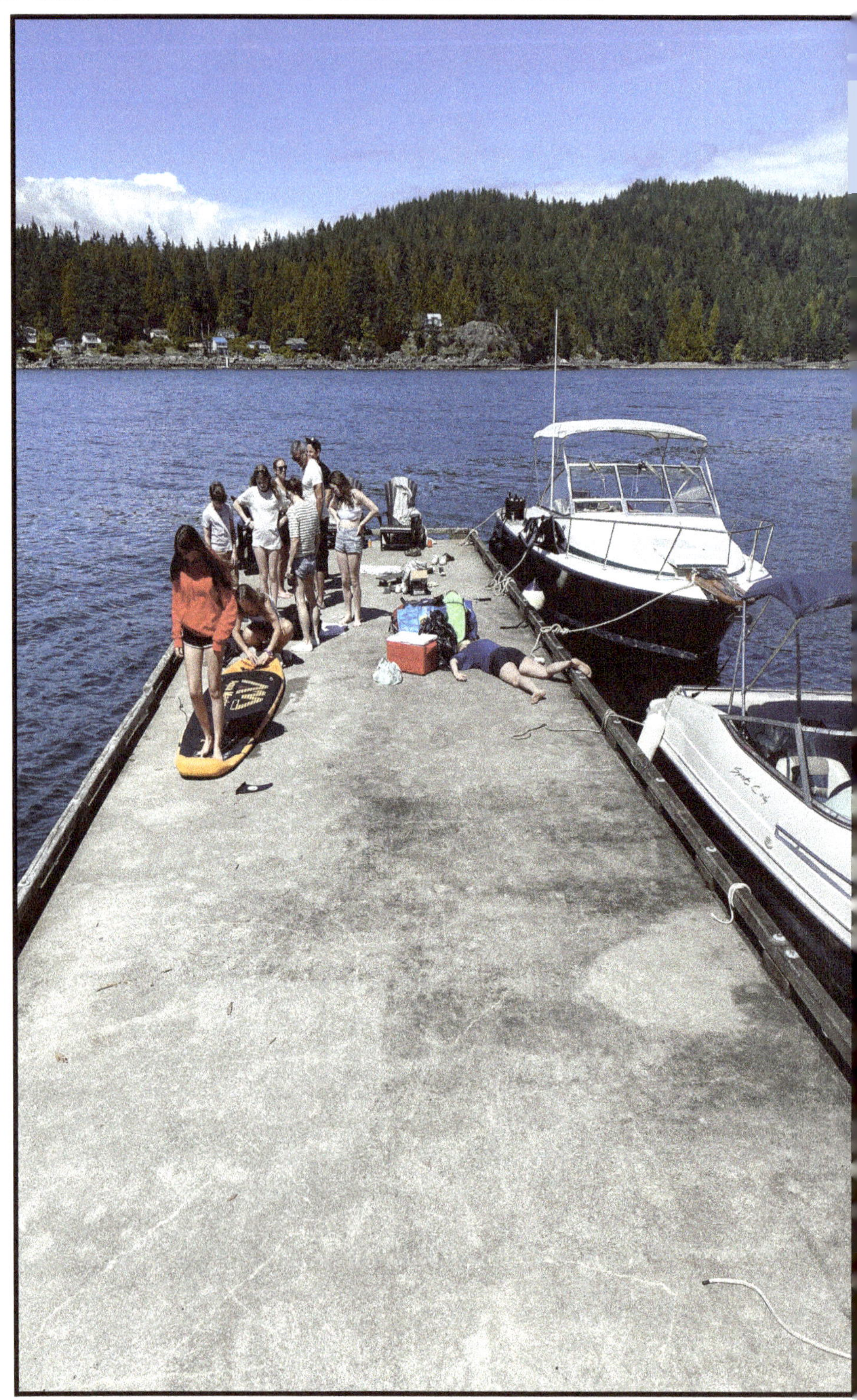

The Complex of Place

Martha Clarkson

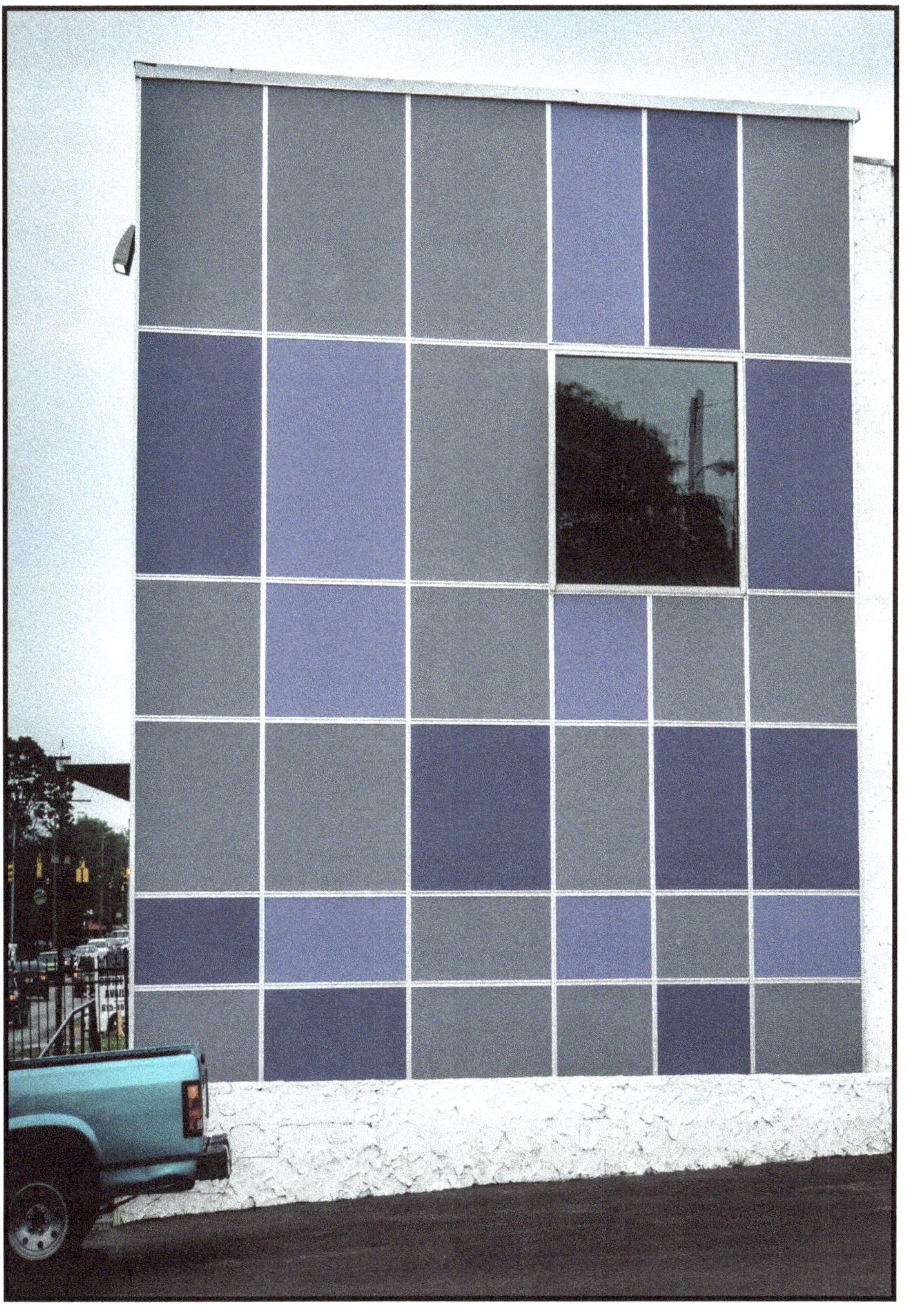

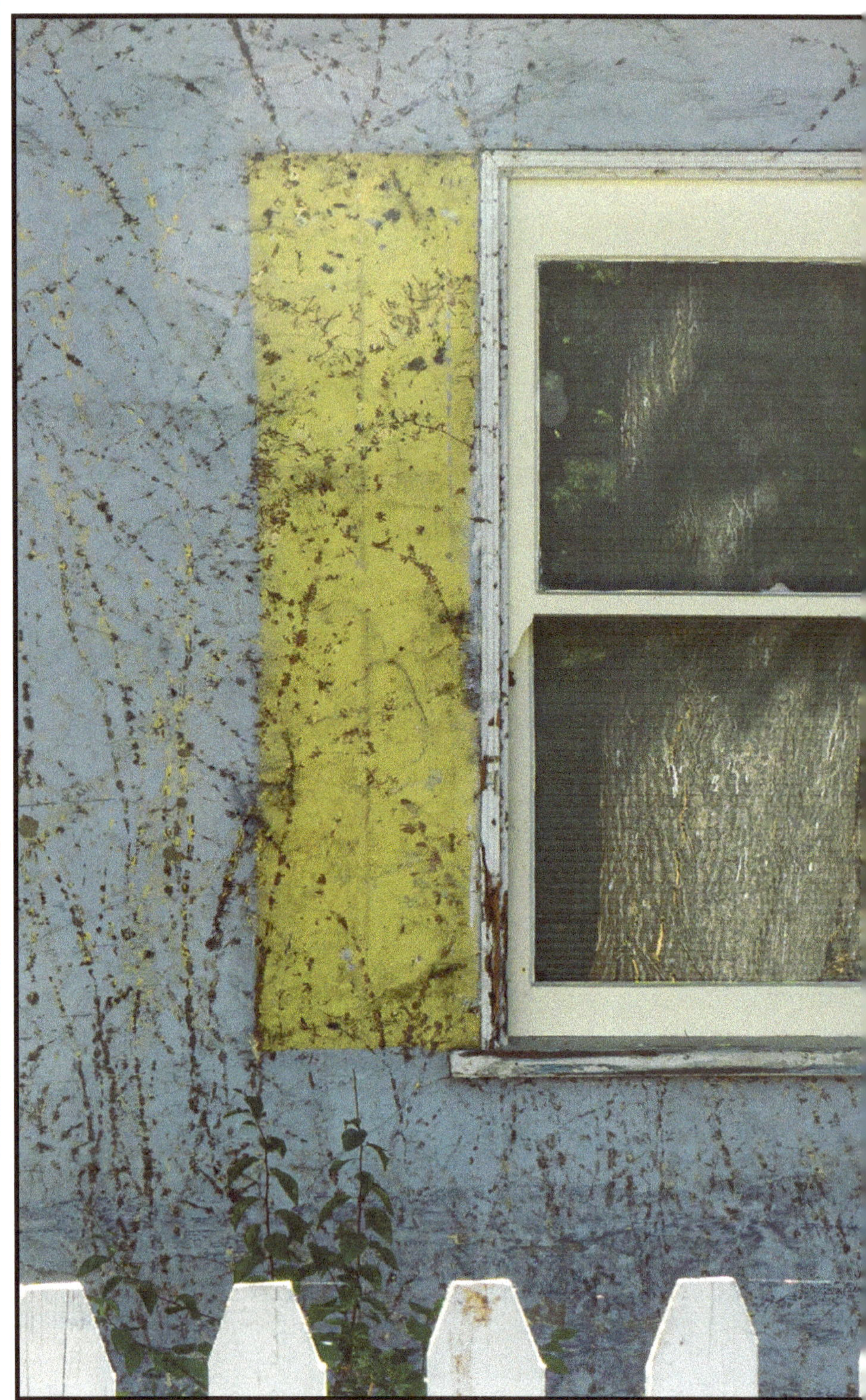

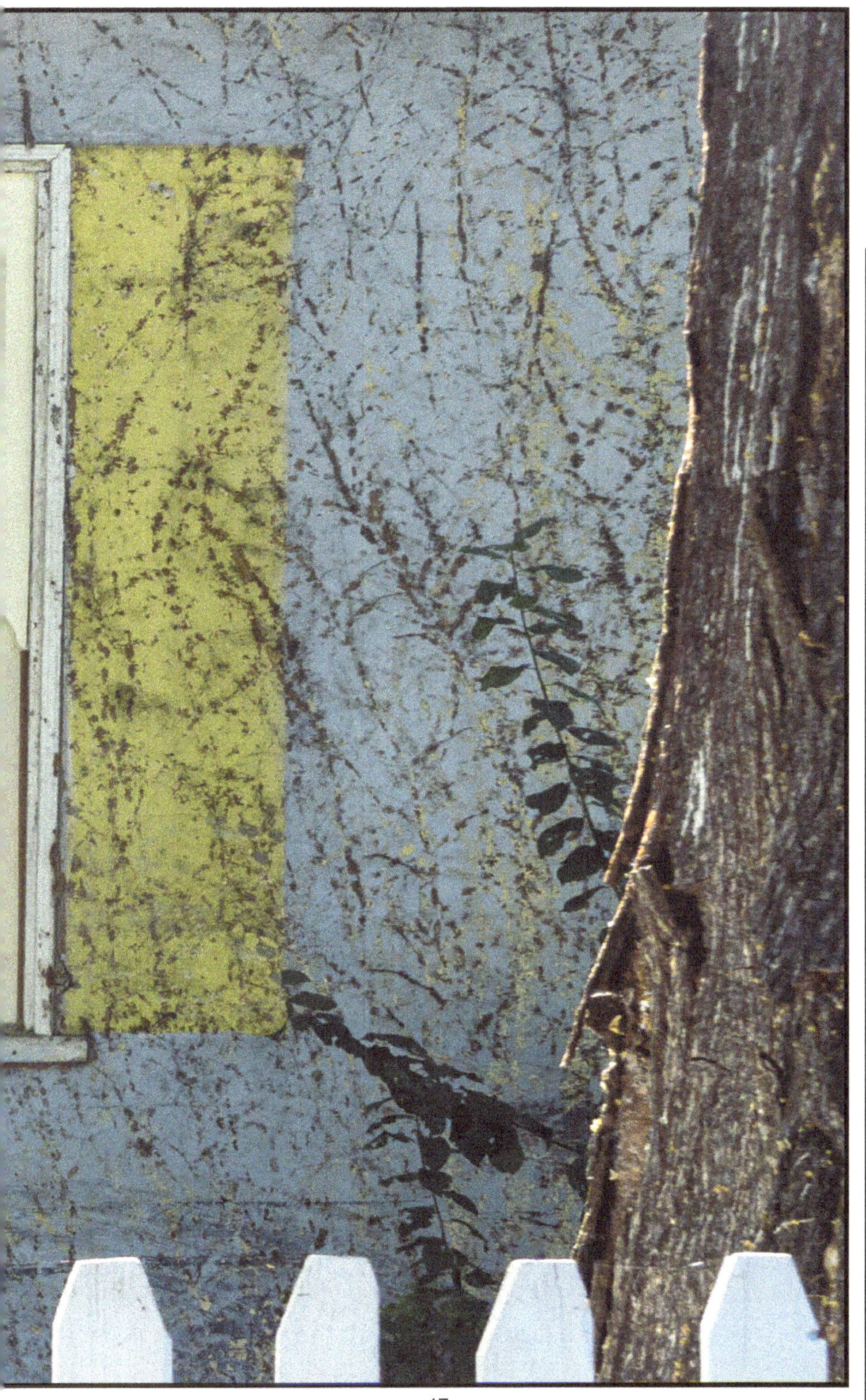

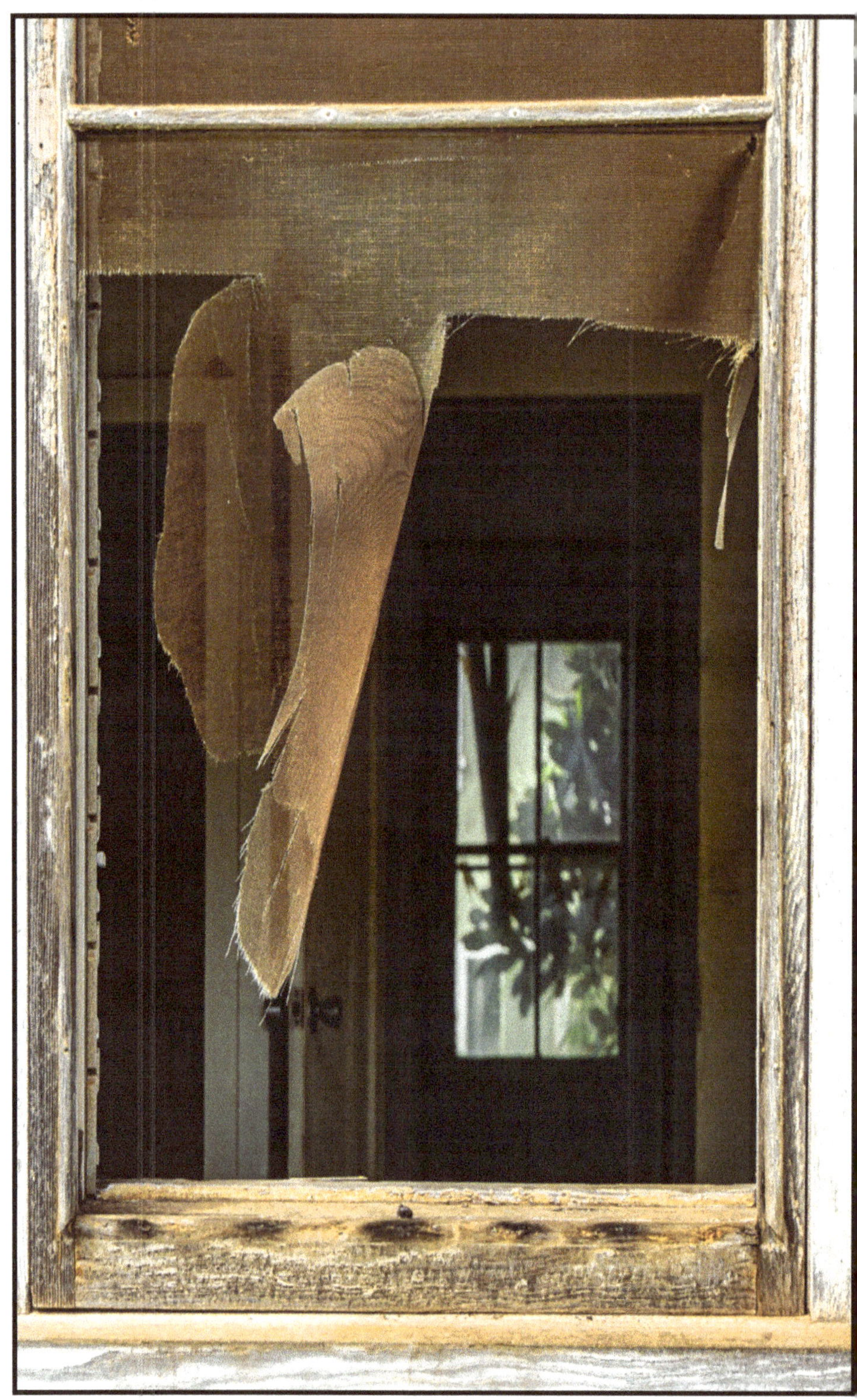

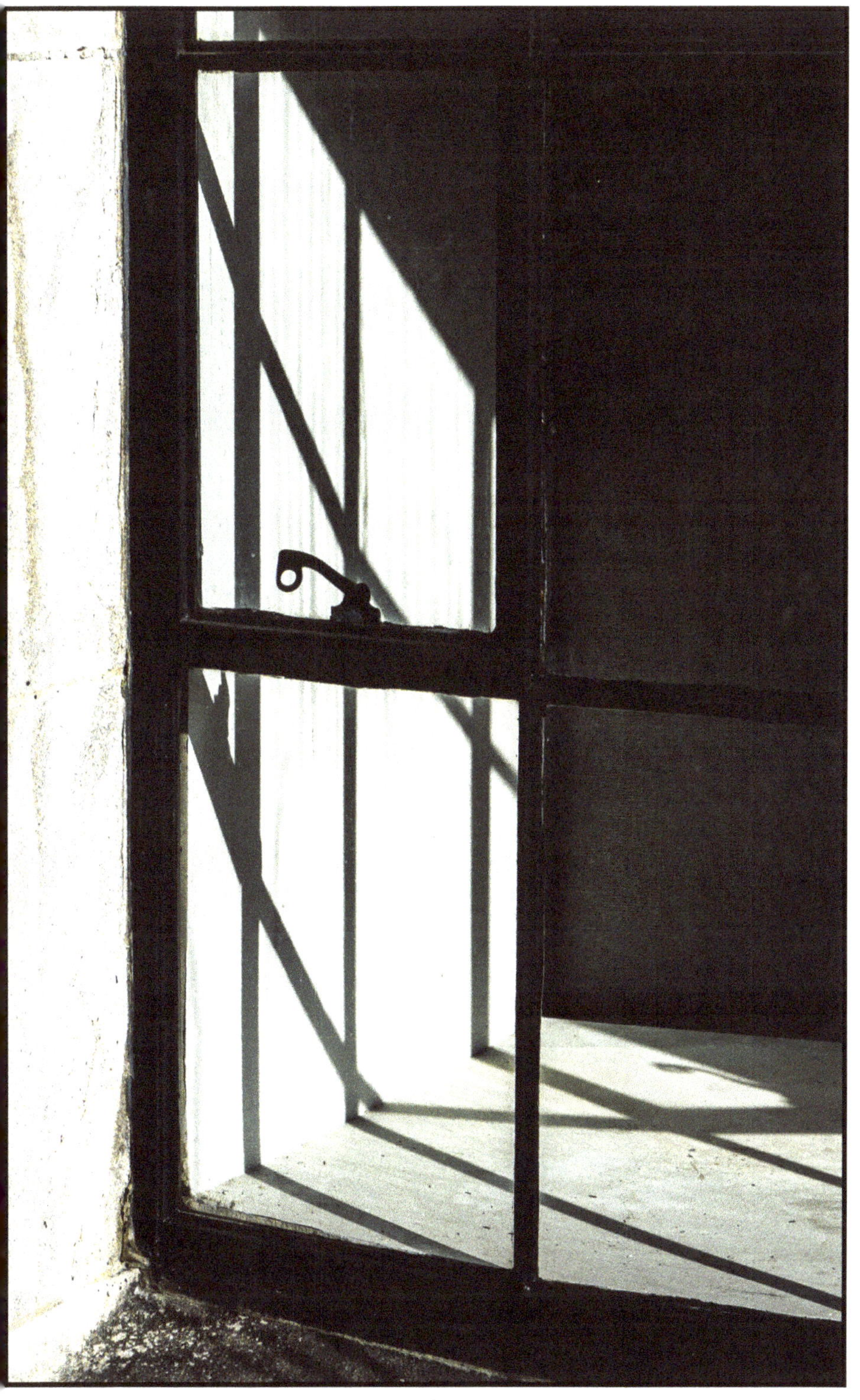

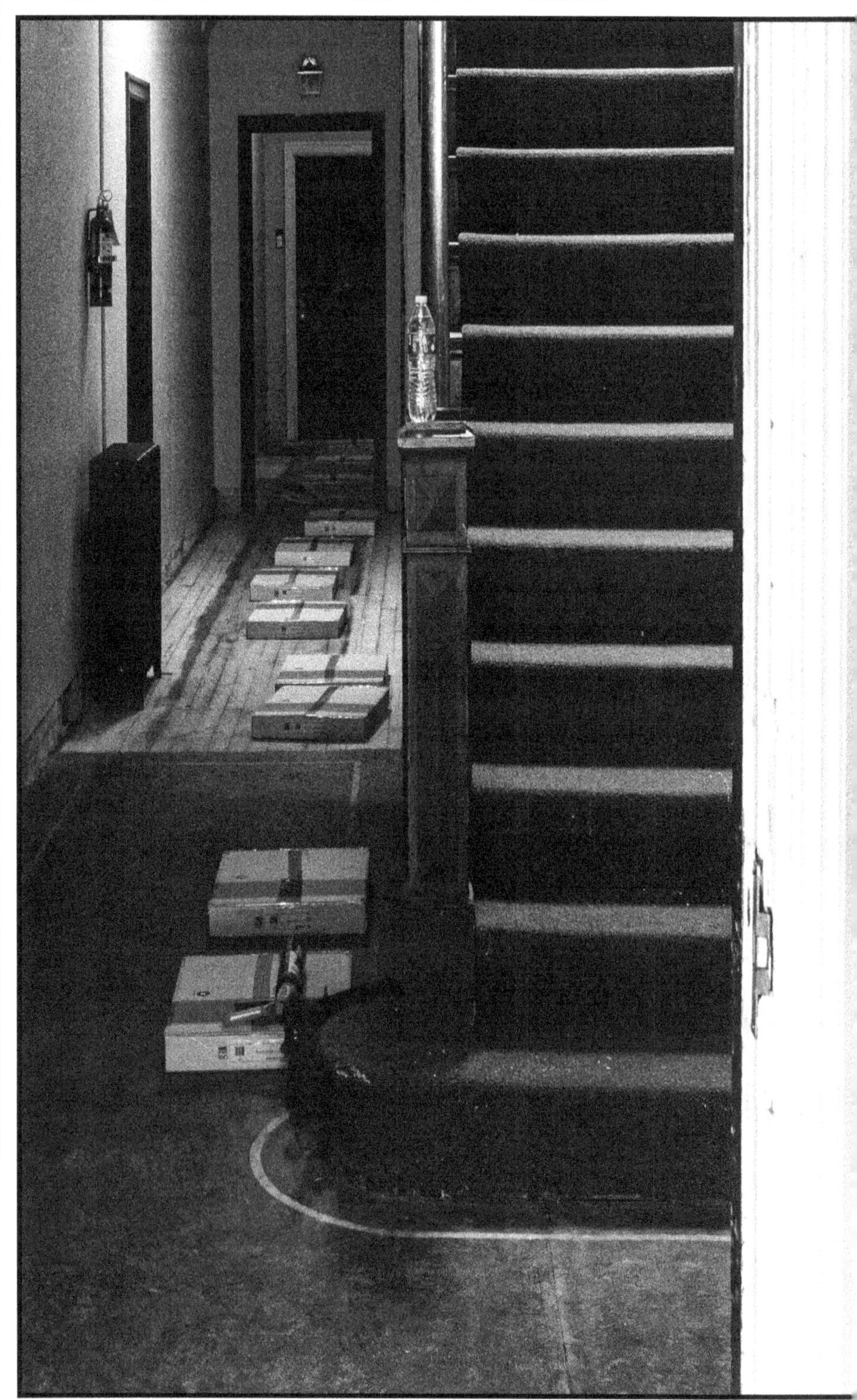

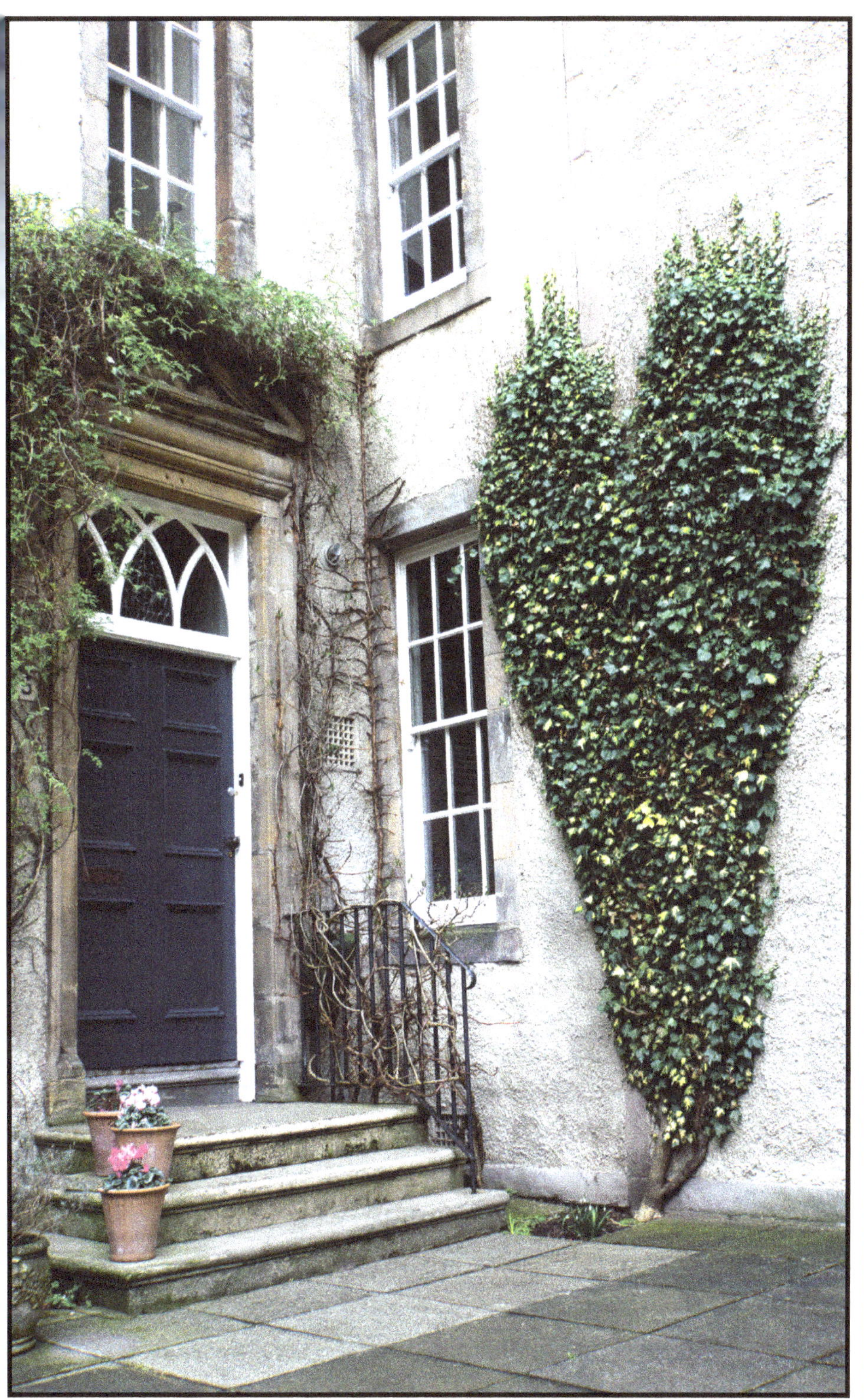

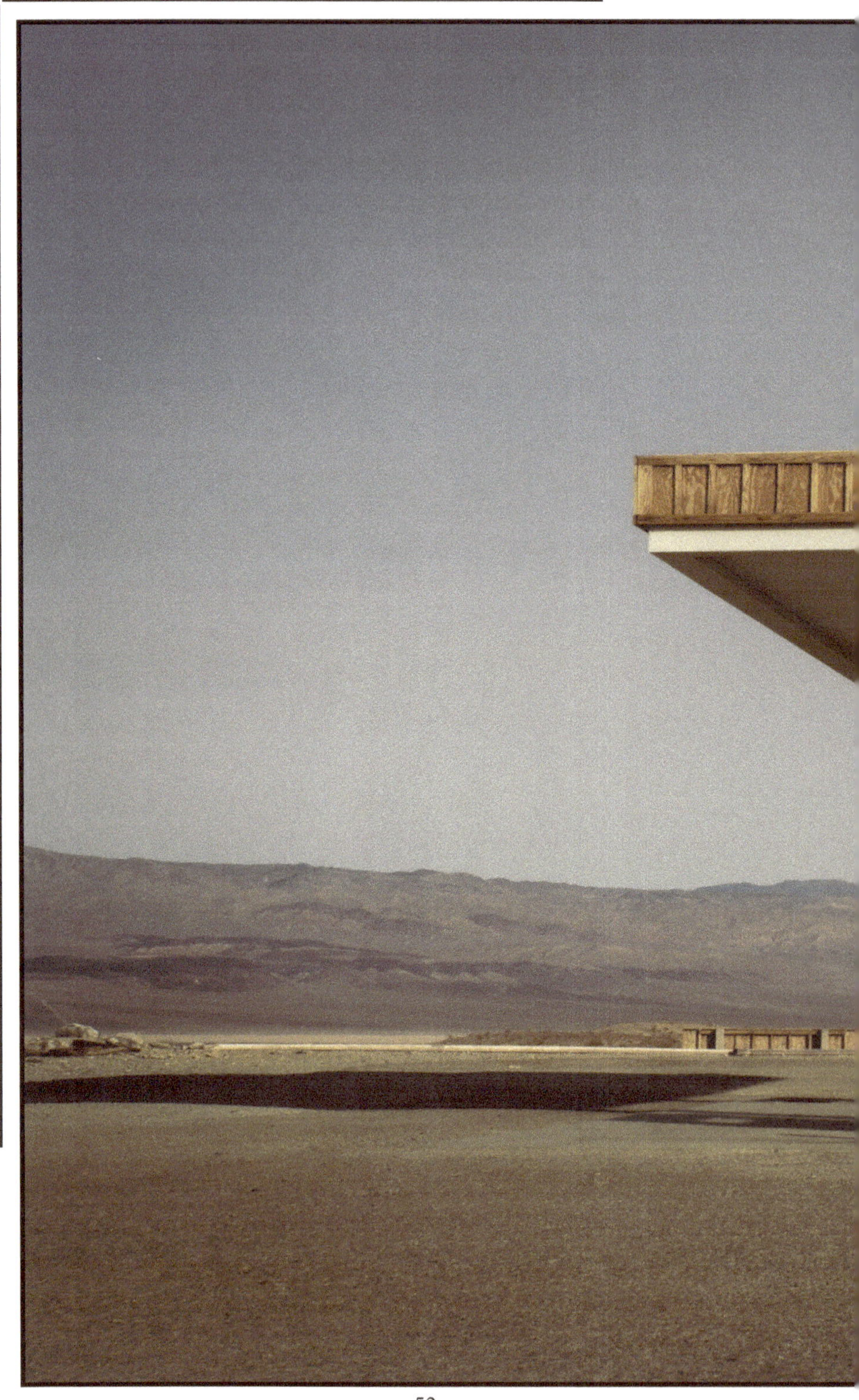

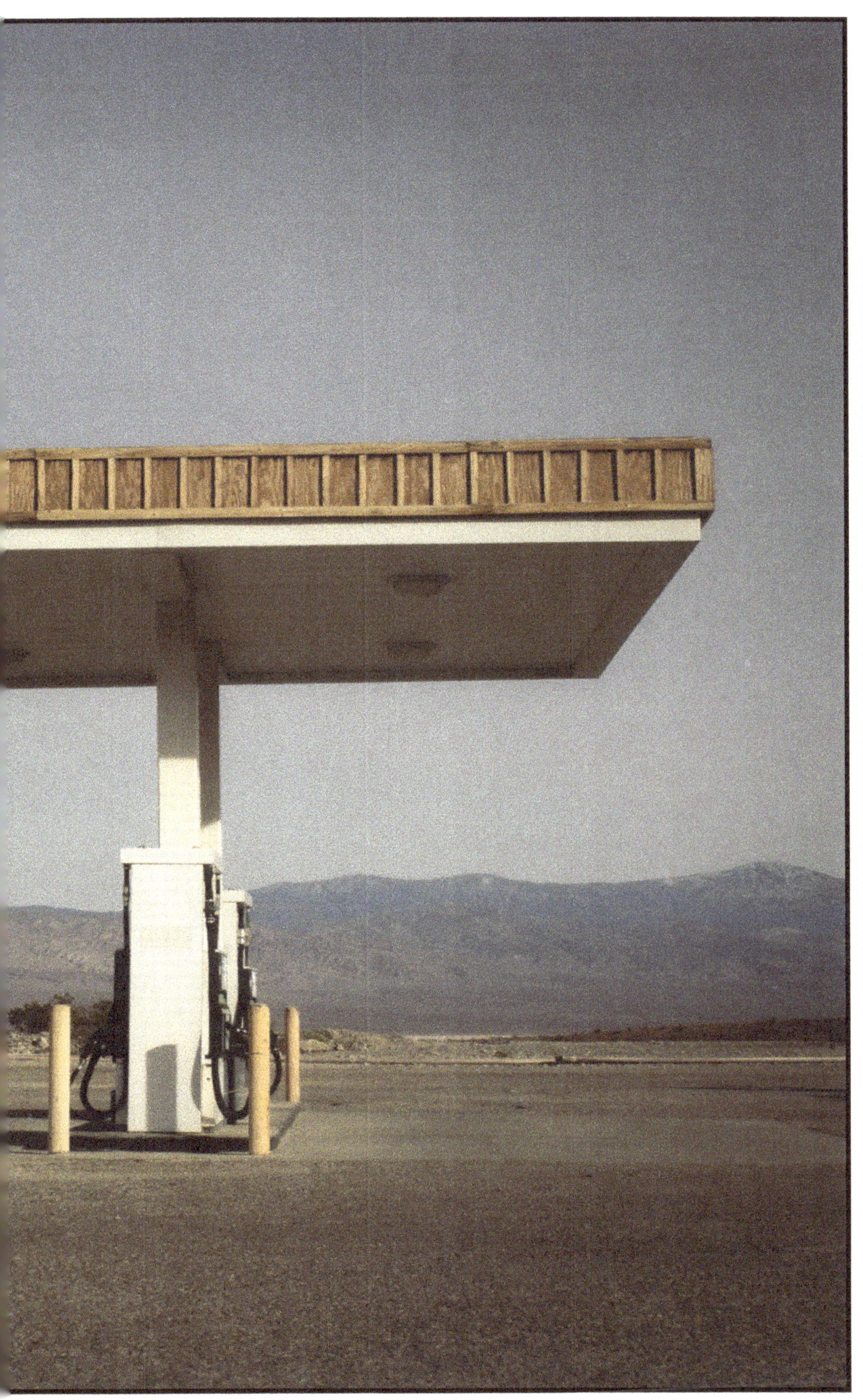

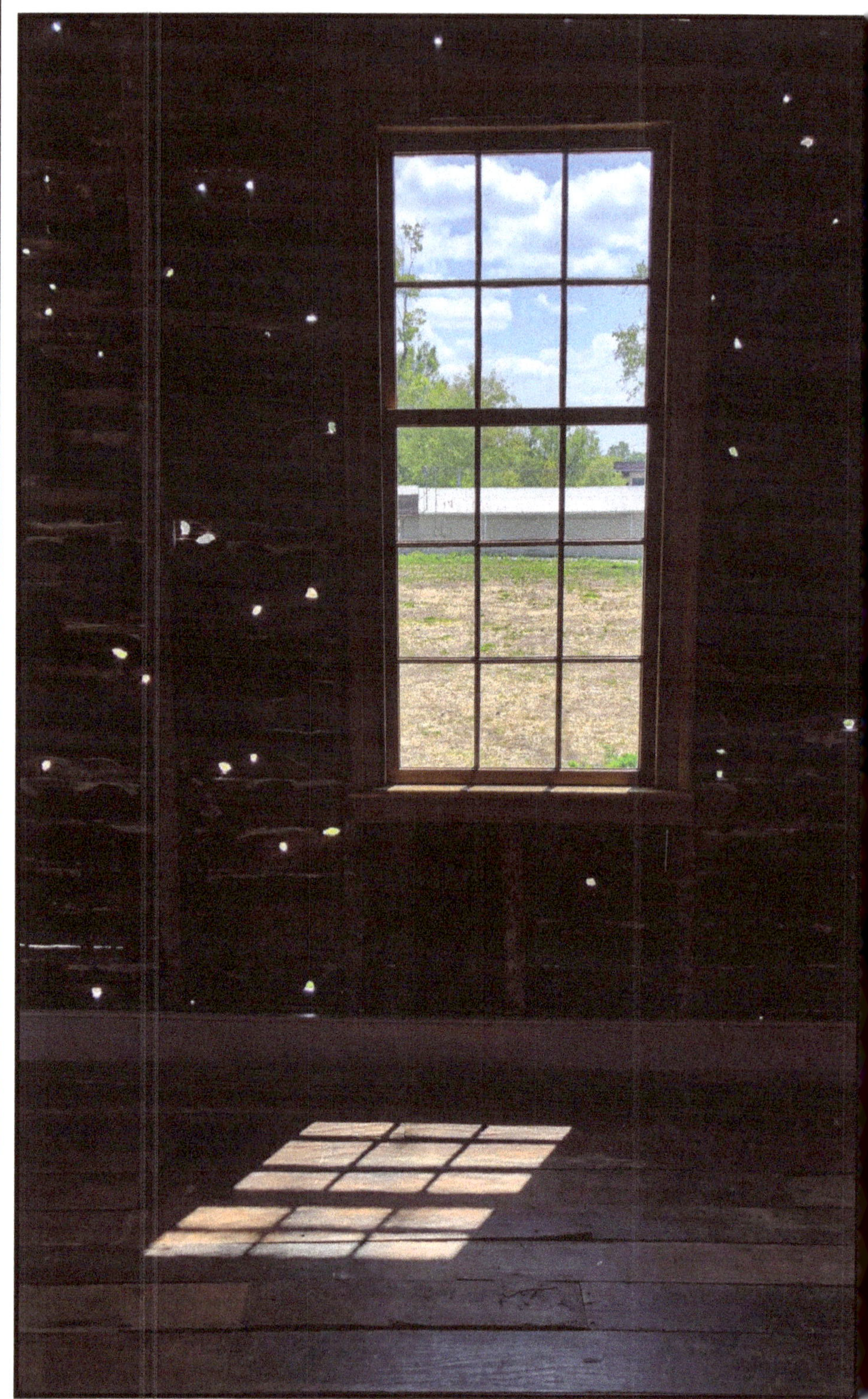

After Branches

Chase Ferree

In nature documentaries, have you ever noticed how plants
make noise? Vines wrap around a helpless trunk or buds emerge
from twigs like paint brush ends until they burst and bloom,
and they sound like creaking leather or hands
across paper. What can be heard when wood grows around
a chain-link fence? Or when the branches work together to lift
the metal barrier's base out of the soil and into the sun? No matter

the path I've taken this week, the flowers themselves
are exceptional. The daily changes from white to pale pink,
sudden deep red leaves turning the whole thing
to purple, magenta. Even when I'm overwhelmed
by my thoughts of the day, the electricity in my ears,
the bascule bridge in relief against the sky, these scents
are so sudden, so urgent. It's as if I have never smelled
a tree before. Underneath these blossoms I burst

into tears as I listen to a daughter say goodbye
to her mother. And yes, I cried last week
when a colleague told another that he loved her, just to say it
out loud, and I can't stop thinking about the mountains—
our mountains—and about the sun, and how even the reflection of its light
is finally warm enough to make me feel my skin. For now, it's March
and someday everything will be back to the way that it was
but better. Better, at least, until the world changes. It always does.
An arborist will cut down a tree, or get sick, or say goodbye
to his daughter, for good this time. If we could slow down
these moments to just the right speed, at last, we would hear

so many little noises.

Surrogate

Beth Curran

I don't know what it's like.
Three babies came easy to me
through a rather quick exchange that startled
the fabric of a marriage.
The process, not so simple.
A grueling 9-month wrench in
a wild girl's heart who thought she could
tame any horse offered.
Before your first child, you asked me to carry for you:
"You birthed three. You can do one more, right?"
I couldn't.
I lost myself to pieces every time
and almost couldn't sew the pieces back together.
You didn't know what it was like.
I know what the first one brought you.
My hand cradling the lump,
insisting it was a defunct milk duct
and not a malignancy.
Then the waiting and the waiting and the waiting.
Now, we wait again.
For months, you didn't tell me
about a woman named Margie on the West Coast.
You see her once a month.
You go to work, take your son to the park,
get a massage, call me while going to Starbucks,
and soon, you will go and pick up your new baby.
Like a vending machine moment. The snap of a very expensive finger.
I wonder what that would have been like—
no morning sickness, no hospital panics, no preeclampsia,
no gestational diabetes, no postpartum sobbing,
no doctor throwing Xanax at my crumpled soul.
What it would be like to say,
"Yes, I'll have what she's having."

[3rd child]

Alina Stefanescu

I discovered absence as
silhouette, the shape of butter-

fly wings missing from my
baby's throat / to exist with-

out this basic engine, a
m/other's failure to grow her just

so, just so the kiss
with which she calls me

[*mommy*], fragile as fractals
in a mind, holding so little yet

culling collapse, a series of frag-
ments / O and the tired bulldog

nextdoor with his imminent
thyroid, snapping, barking /

Who can belief this life, a bed's
noisy pansies, powerless

a few things to remember

Connor Doyle

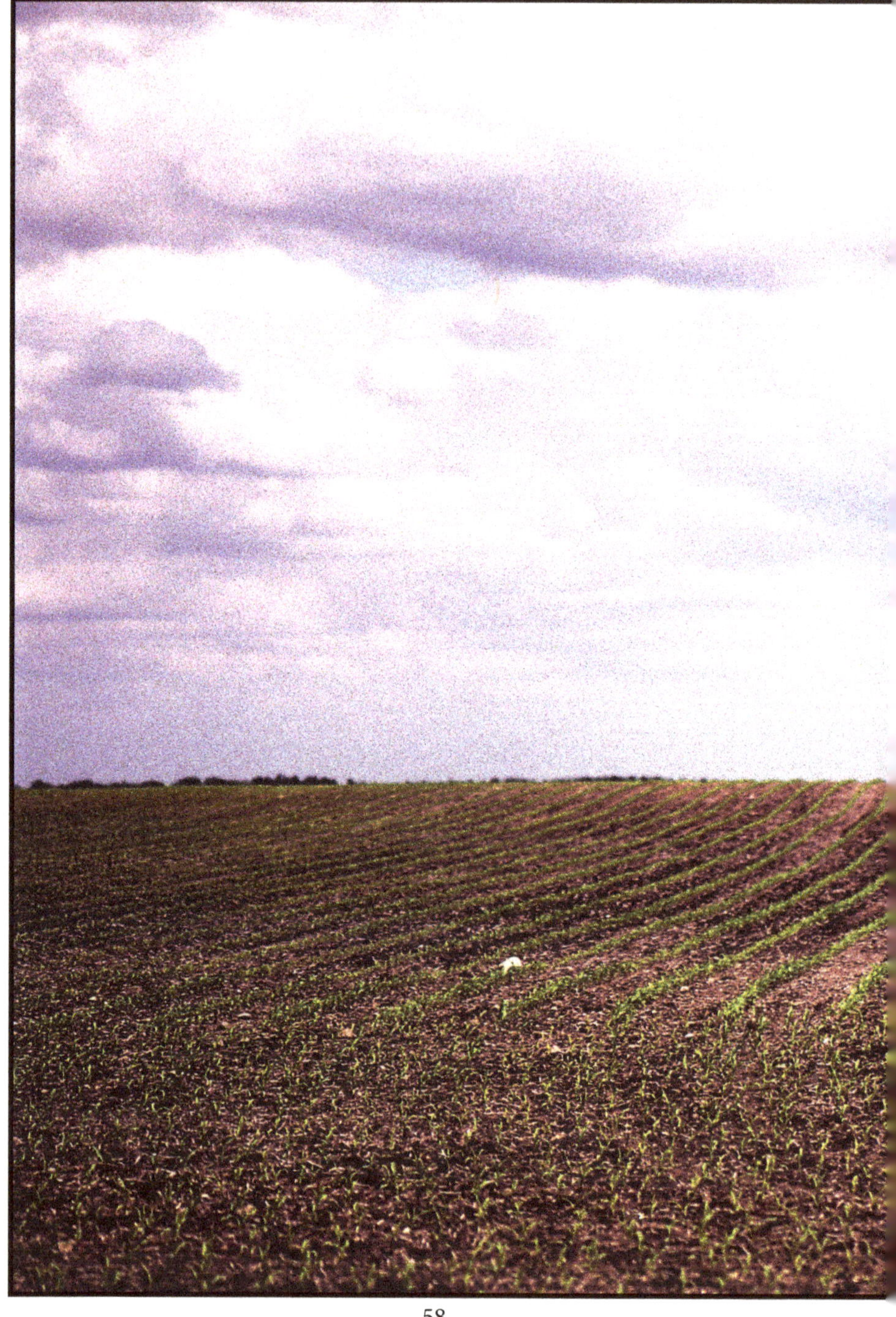

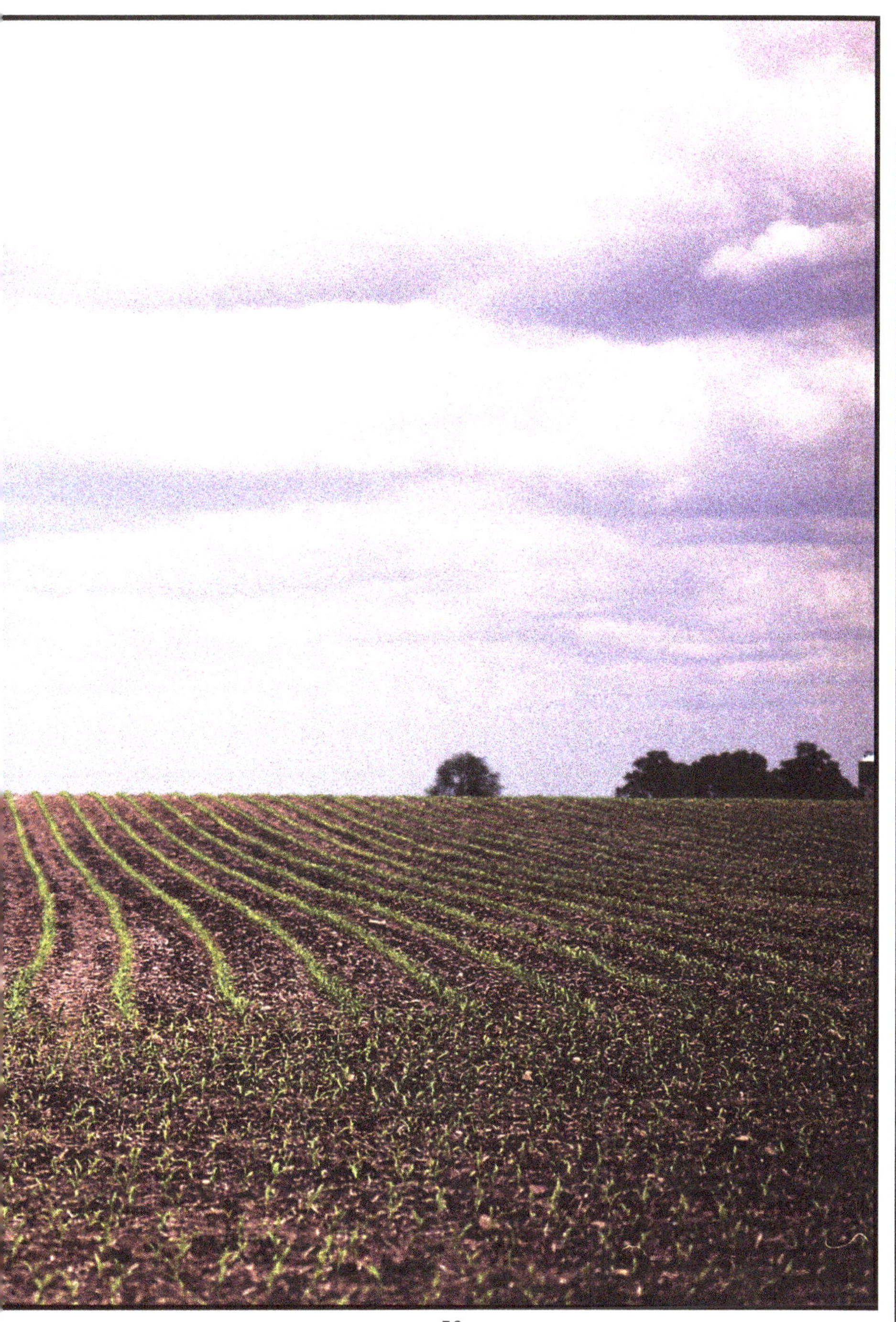

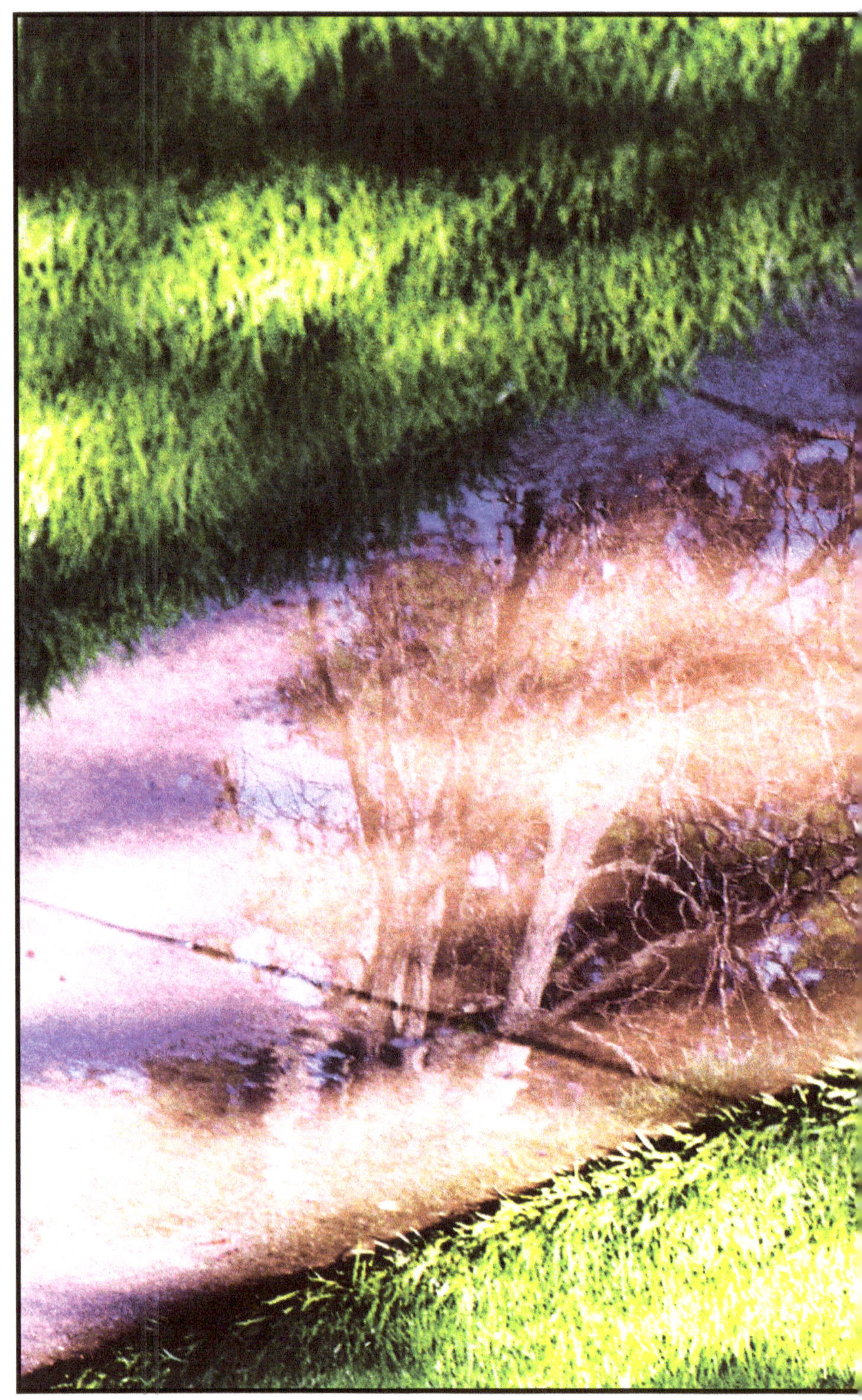

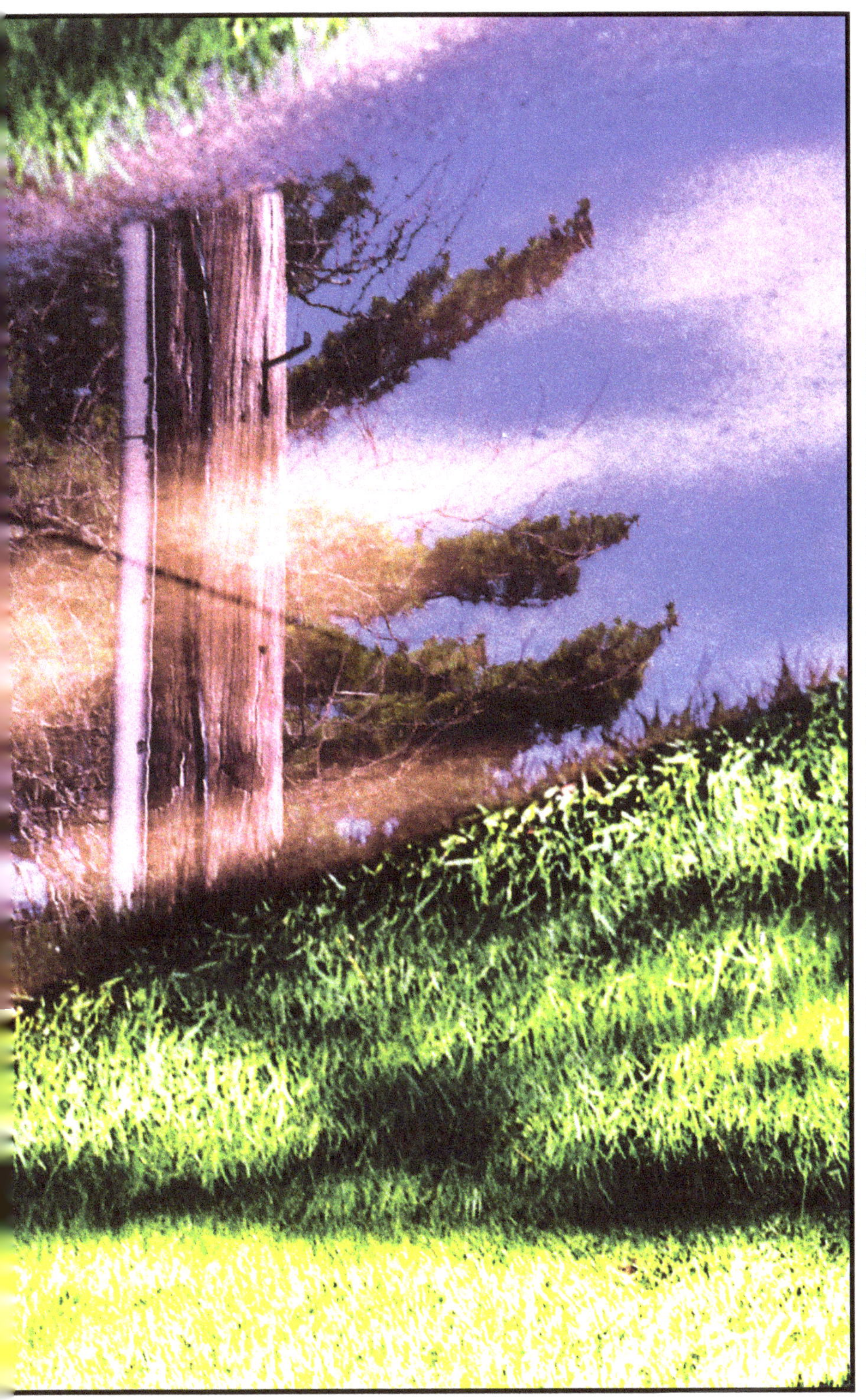

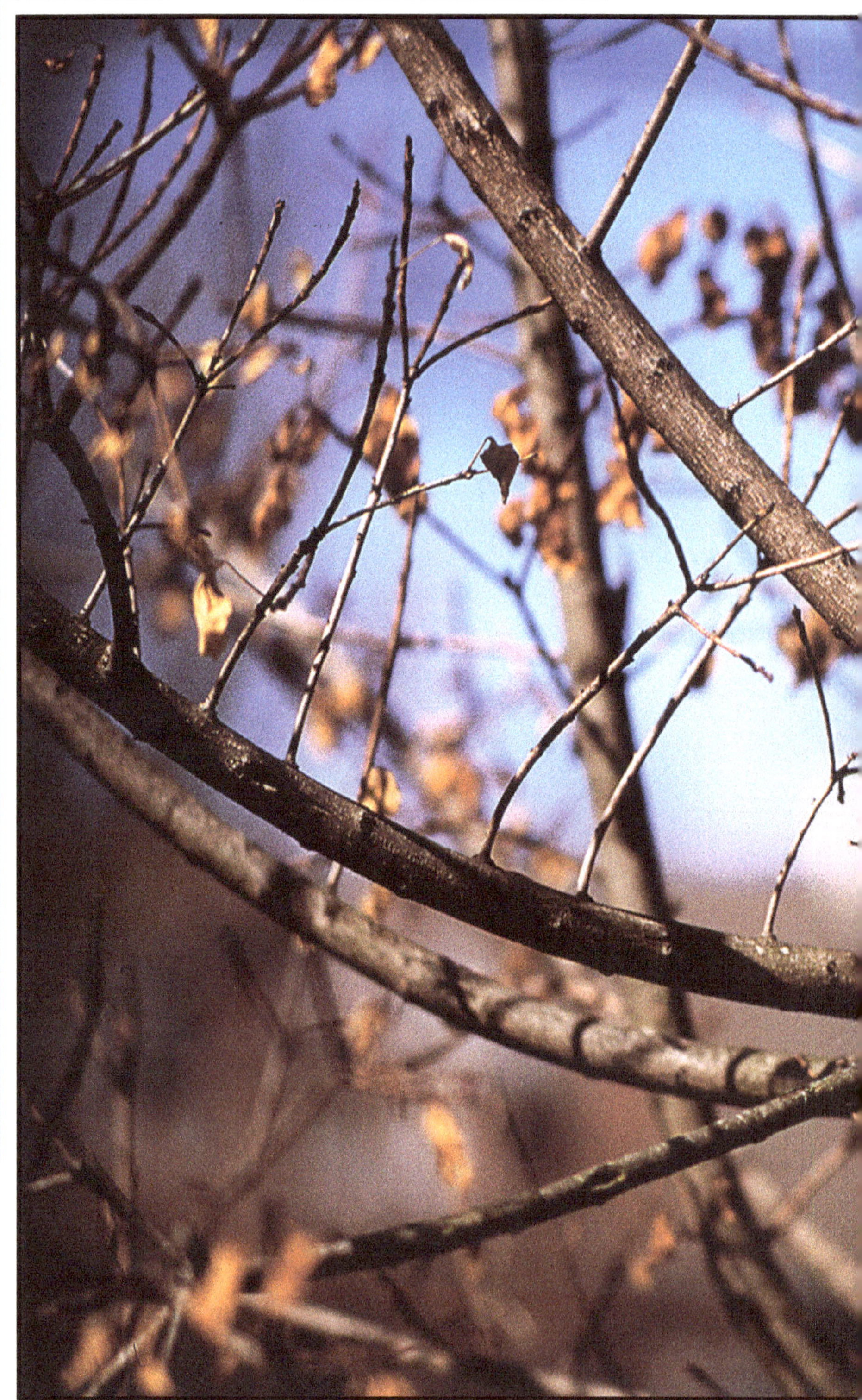

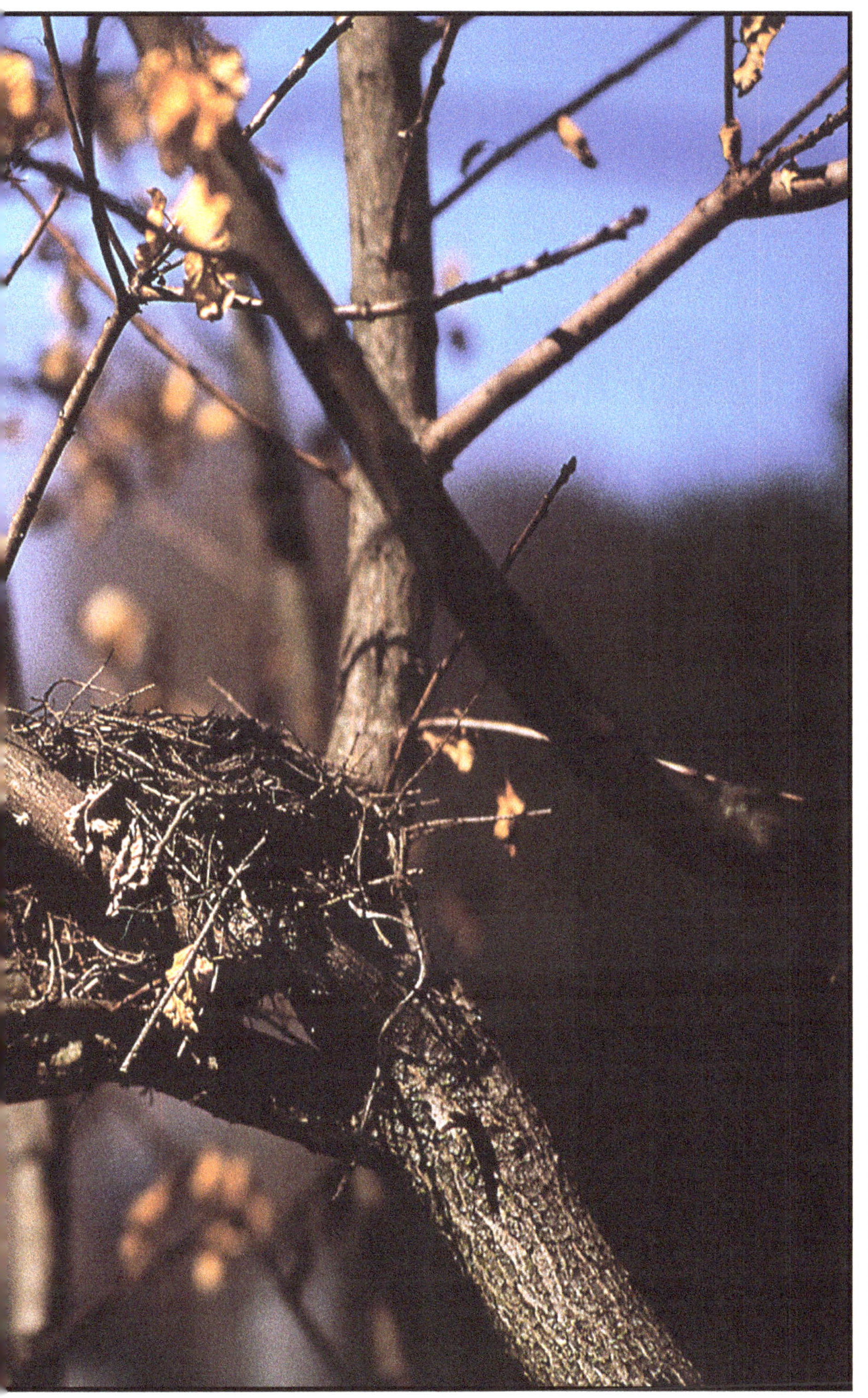

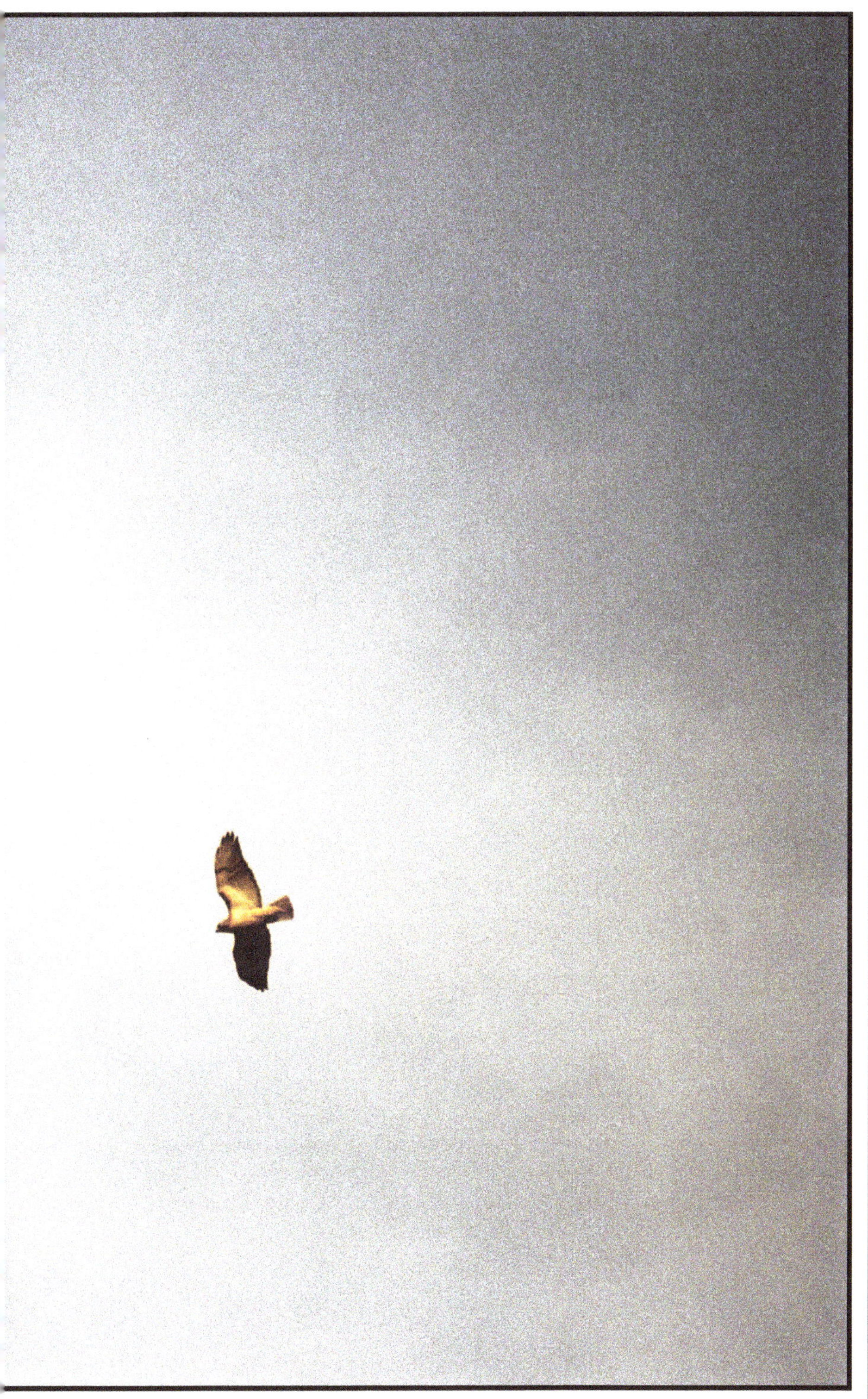

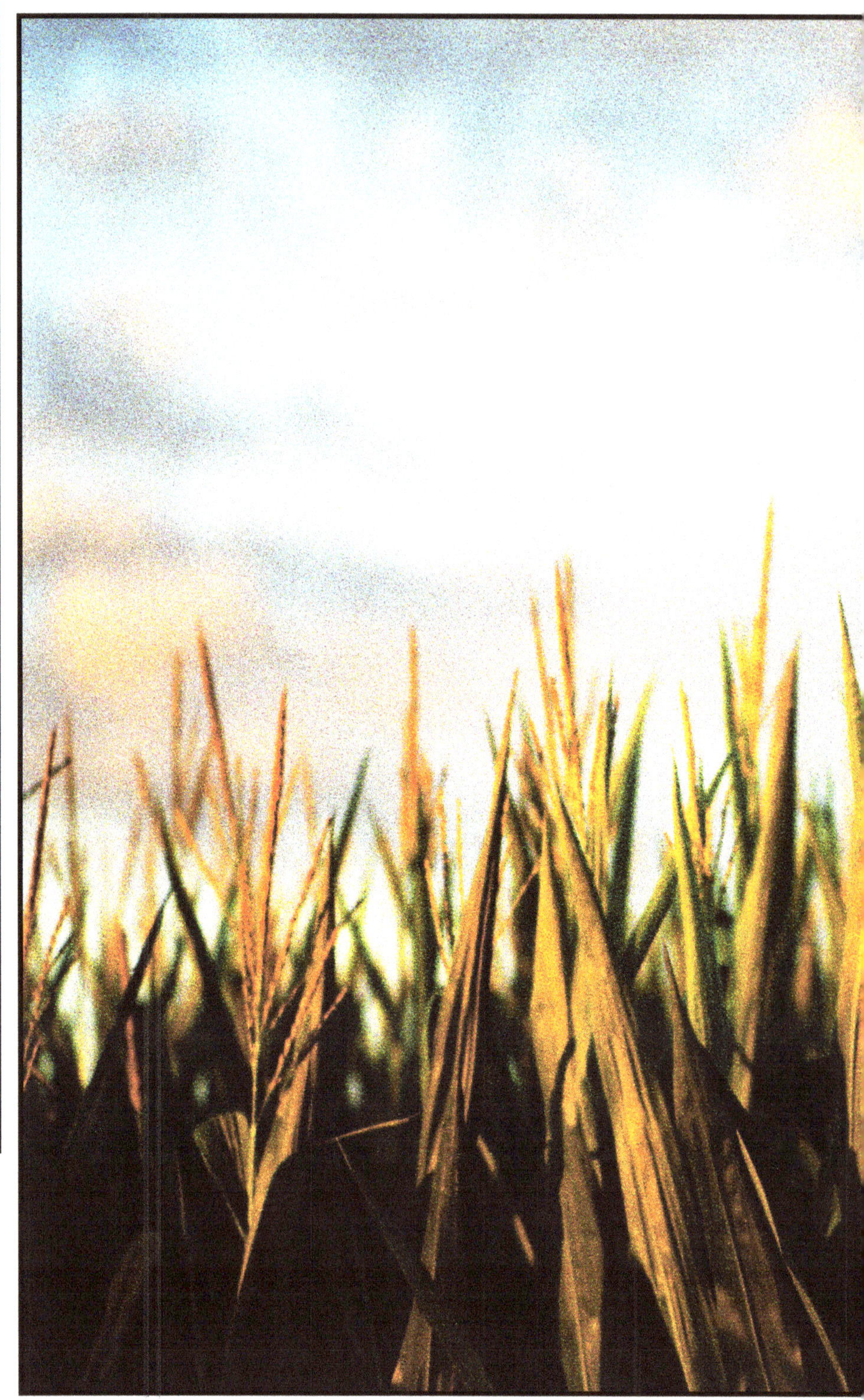

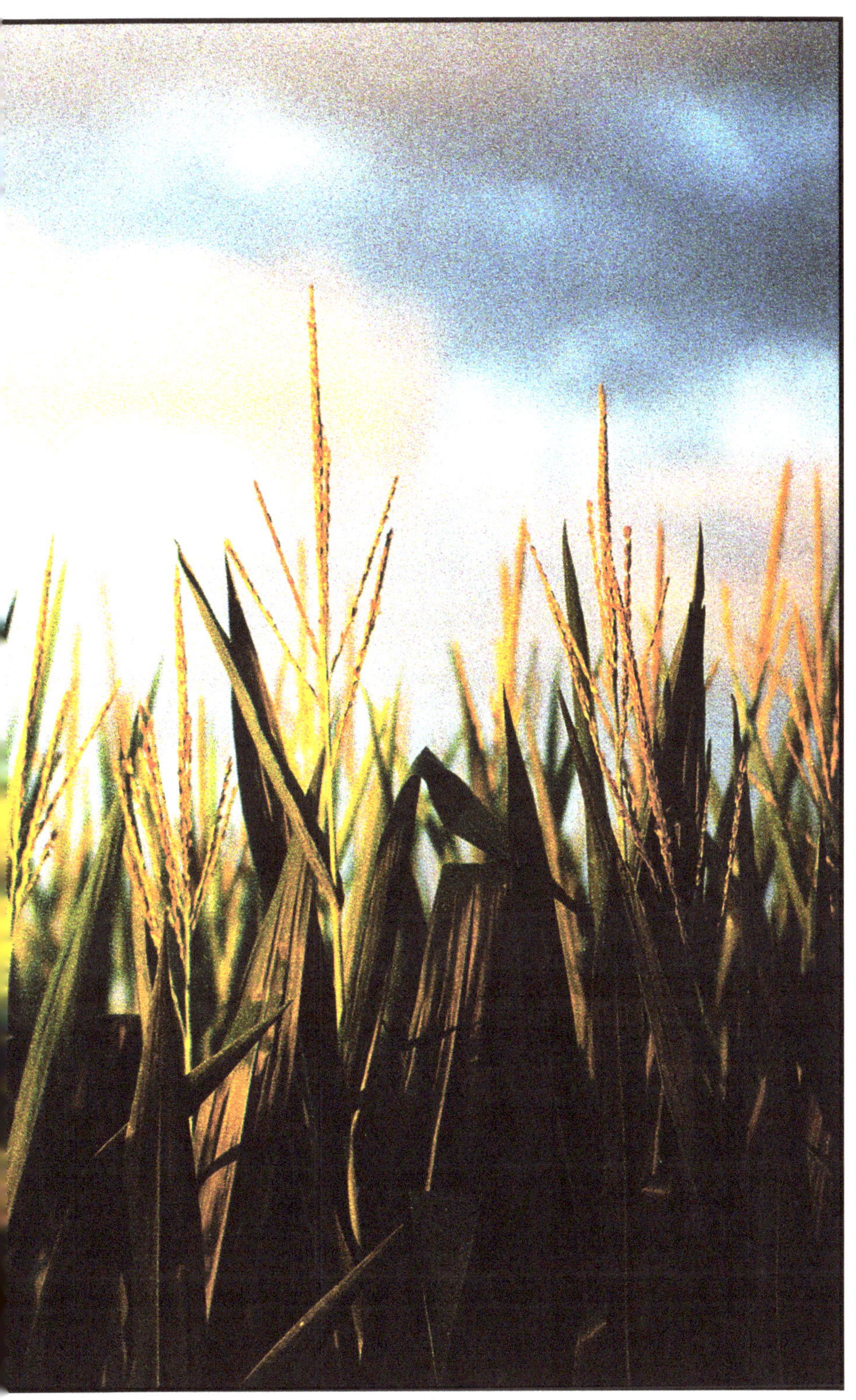

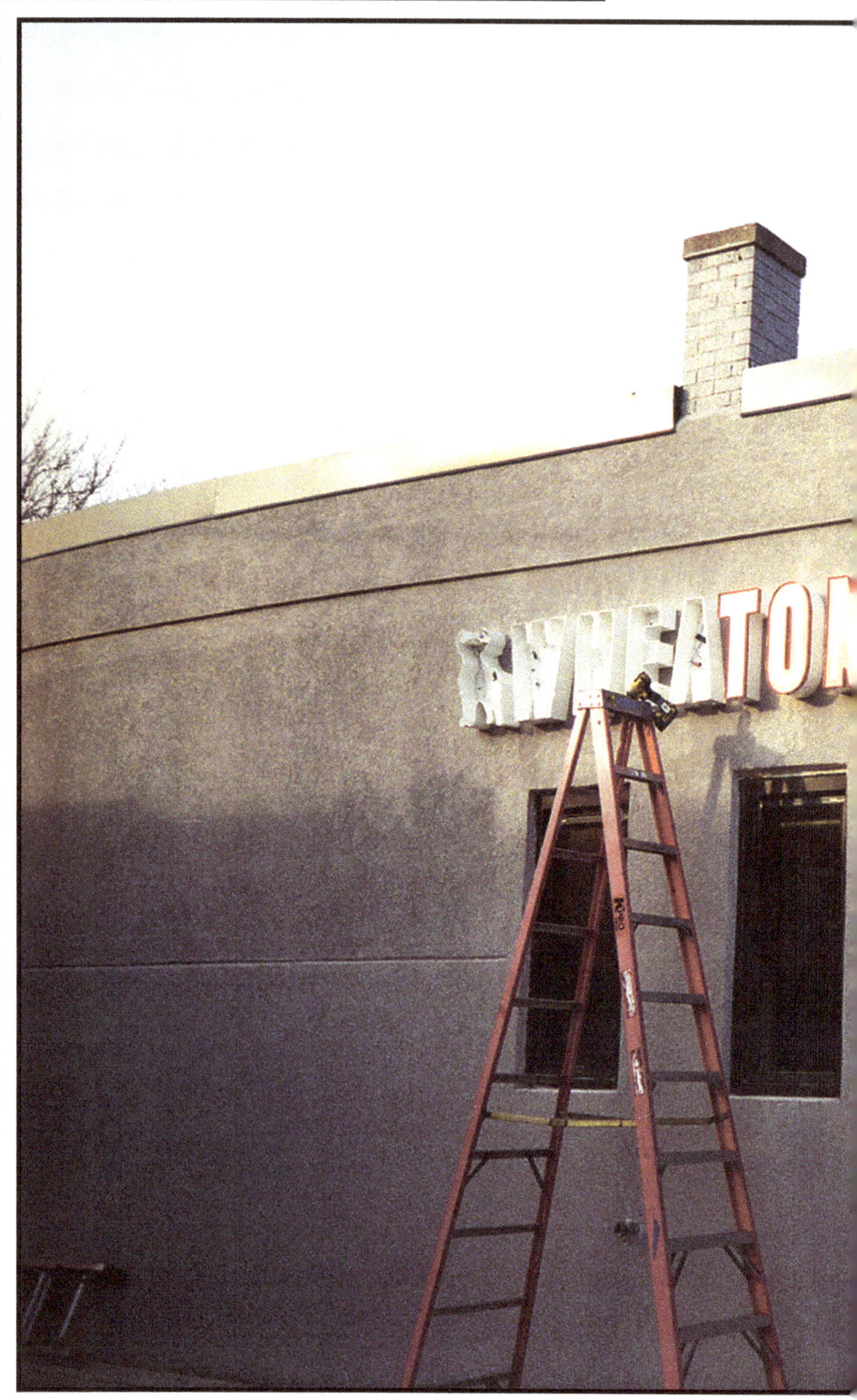

RW WEATO

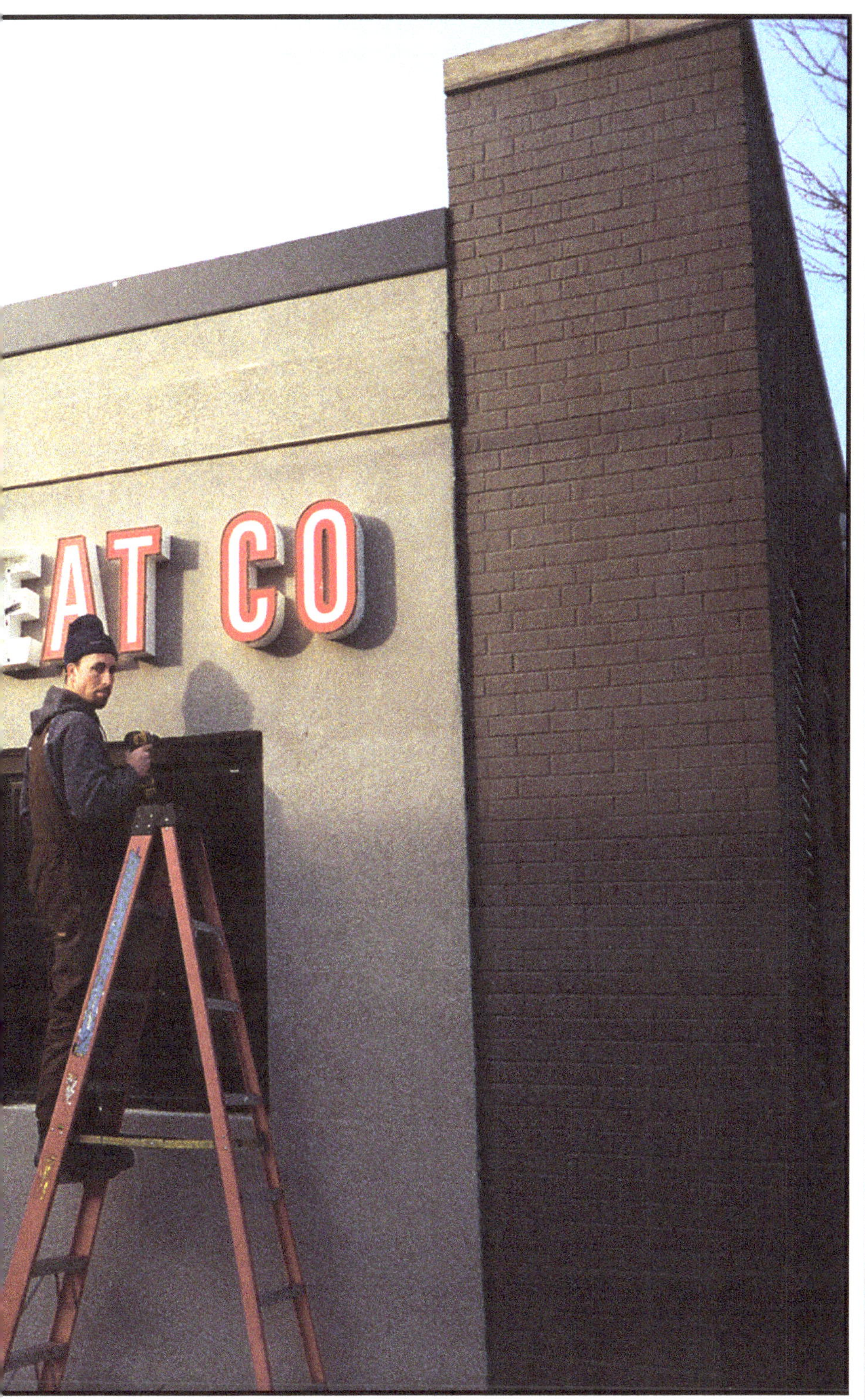
EAT CO

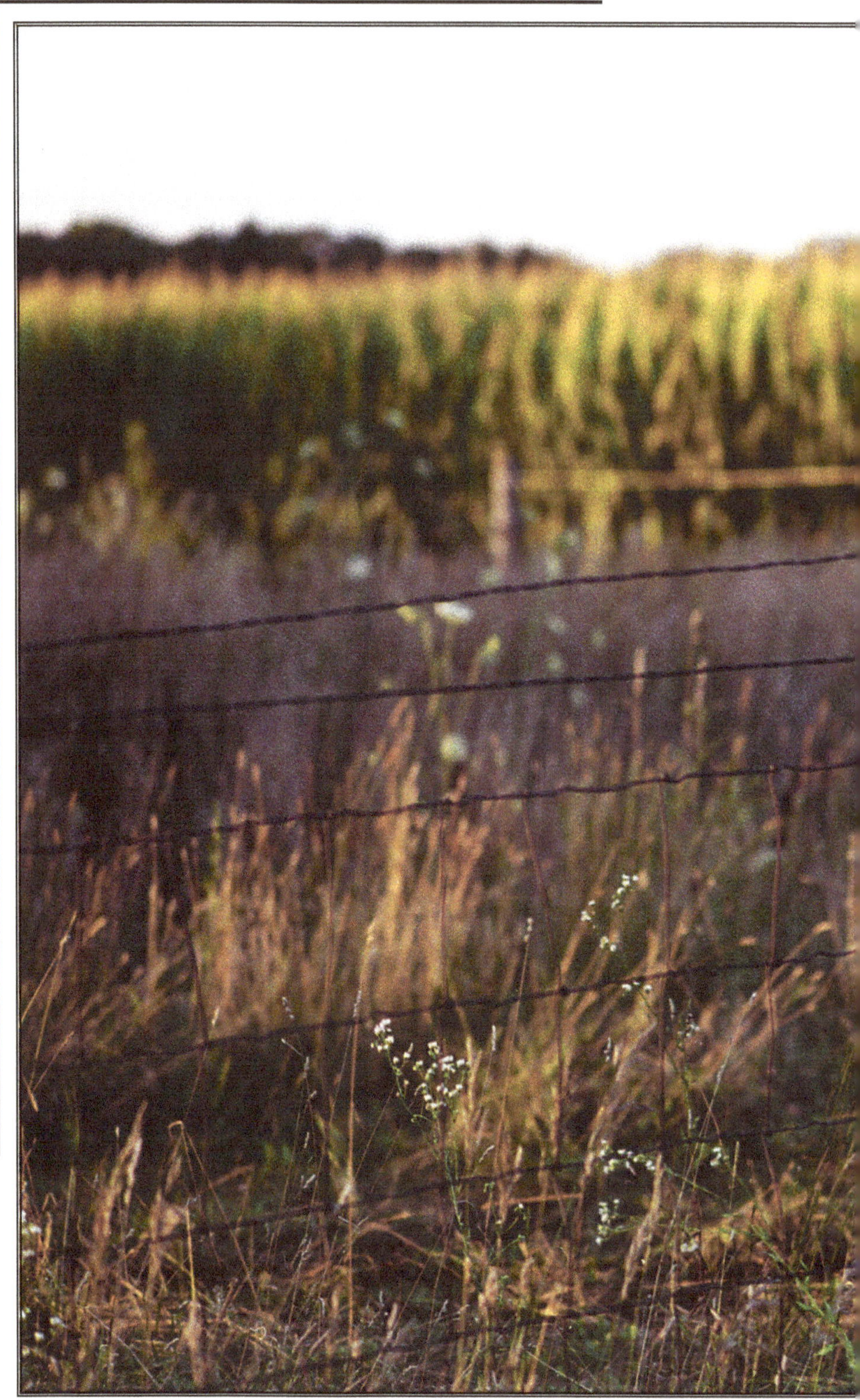

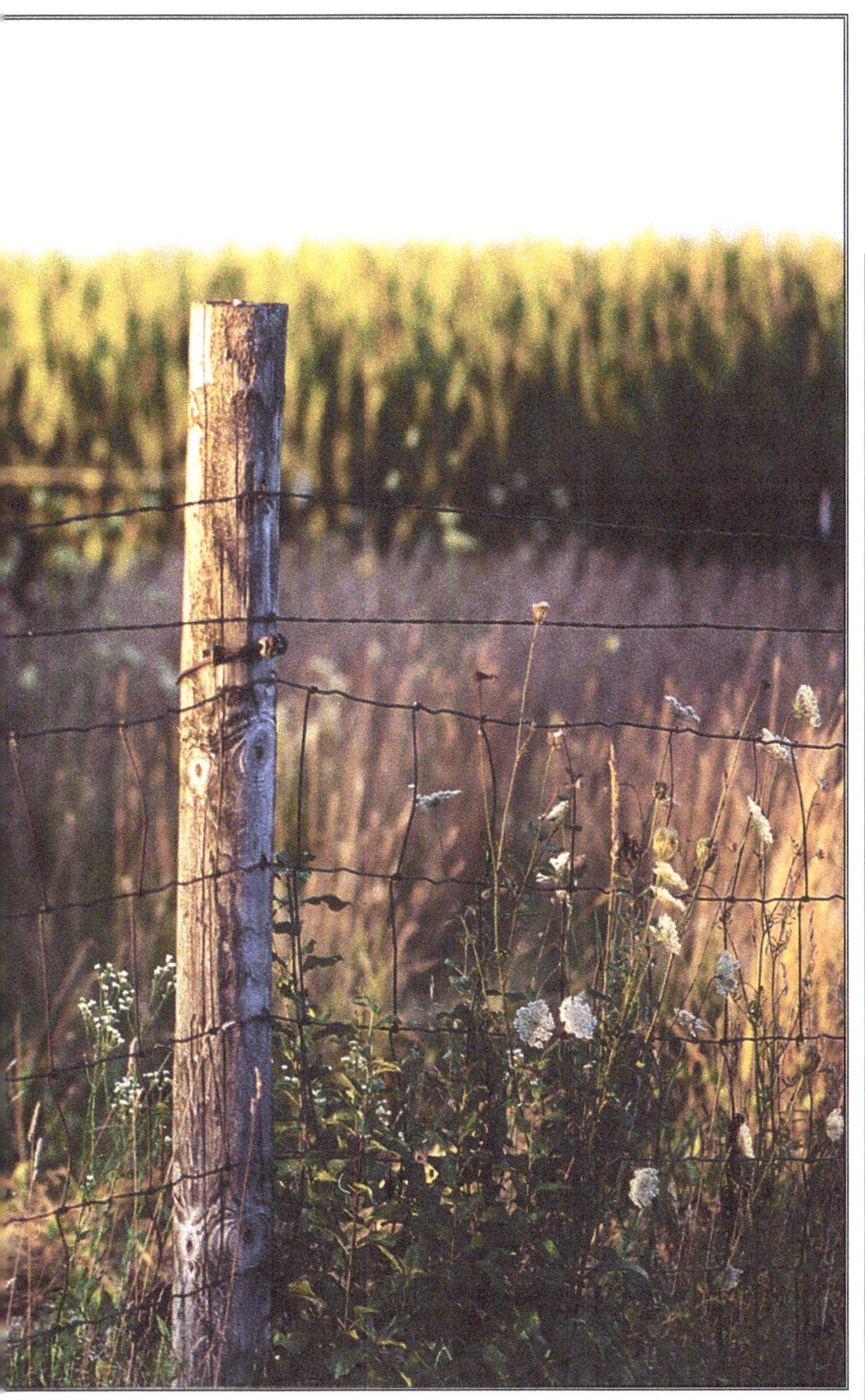

Faith By The Side Of The Road

Dig Wayne

rushin' t'the down believin',

tryin' ta make sense-a-beans.

golden blood spills on waves of injustice.

spit in the ditches of heaven, birthin' clouds of mud.

can't see my hand before me, reachin' out empty;

'cept for hope prints in the tender palm.

dangerous times ta be rubbed wrong by somethin' ya can't even see.

grim totals lie in the sallow eyes by a truth undone.

pull me up by my godly misgivings, heave the devil outta me.

straddle fiction, fate and fibbery all down the line.

glutton for a dramatic finish, apparitions troll hard wires.

a tasteless butter-tongue drops anchor and drags up what once was suspiciously laid ta rest.

wrapping guardrails in padded rooms that don't believe.

golden blood spilling on waves of injustice due ta fear of the inevitable.

Ode to Philtrums

Lauren Kalita

1. Max Ernst's self-portrait Punching Ball collage, 1920, recto, p. 353
    a. the philtrum's shadowed concavity dips into a long thin line of upper lip, is echoed by crevassed line down the middle of the leafy transparency of a lower lip
    b. to say nothing of the tautology of the long straight liquid line of that grandiloquent nose above it all & dividing two absolute eyes set in yin-yang quartz & tourmaline quadrants presided over by one immaculate forehead – a poet's forehead? who can say – w/2 discreet lines forming a symmetry w/the stripes of the bow tie holding the head to the body which correspondence undoes me
    c. the philtral groove – sigh
2. Max Beckmann's self-portrait as a Clown, 1920, verso, p. 352
    a. the insouciant nose, full up w/foreboding bravado, indicates a teardrop philtrum that imposes itself upon the upper lip, creates the cavity that bows the mouth
        i. his heavily lidded eyes make bright arrows of intention
3. de Chirico, recto, p. 357
    a. secrets the seeds of his own sublimity in a vaginal philtrum, engorged all around
    b. slits the difference
        i. w/his good right hand balancing the calipers of long shapely digits
            1. self-portrait 1925 (did I mention?)
    c. the profundity of de Chirico's commissures create chasms
        i. buccal rivulets carry the run-off of unspoken paroxysms of amor fati
            1. they run parallel to but never quite meet his reduced mentolabial furrow
                a. & who knows what secrets he keeps to himself there, rolled up tight in epidermal scrolls unopened
IV. Ellen Day Hale, 1885, verso, p. 272
    A. implied philtrum, keeps company with the pre sumptuous proboscis[1]
    B. in constant conversation, maintaining a condescending distance from the vermilion border[2]
        a. mutual mistrust as though the one organ would reveal the secrets of the other, inevitably misinterpreting in the telling

---

[1] Proboscis, noun – the nose of a mammal, especially when it is long & mobile such as the trunk of an elephant or the snout of a tapir
- In entomology – (in many insects) an elongated sucking mouthpart that is typically tubular & flexible
- In zoology – (in some worms) an extensible tubular sucking organ

[2] Vermillion border, noun – the pigmented edge or zone or the carmine margin of the upper lip

b. a steady synesthetic stream inhaled

    i. the cavum oris [3] carping cant capriciously about the snout

    ii. insuperable nares [4] lording above it

C. a cane dangles from her wrist just below the protruding pisiform [5]

    c. the cane continues all the way to the bottom of the frame (ahem, the *canvas*)

        i. the cane is not in alignment with the lines of nose & abbreviated philtrum

        ii. the skin-colored cane is off to the side

        iii. in fact I do not believe there ever was a cane but that Ellen invented it, peripherally

        iv. the cane is an aside, telling us something on the sly...

        v. her impossibly long hand whiter than necessary against the expanse of black shag fingers tucked in withholding leading away

        vi. I want to grab her by her ear handles & kiss her full on the mouth, nose to nose

V. Aurelia De Sousa 1900, verso, p. 308

    A. a through line from her part through the glabella [6] down the expanse of a spiritually daunting nose

        i. with derring do jump off the upturned dorsum [7] into the perfectly symmetrical slalom of her profound philtrum

        ii. let the begrudging bow shoot you

---

[3] Cavum oris, Latin, noun – buccal cavity, oral fissure, mouth

[4] Nares, noun - nostrils

[5] Pisiform, noun – a small rounded carpal bone situated where the palm of the hand meets the outer edge of the wrist
- though Ellen's pisiform protrudes protractedly, did it worry her with arthritic intent, vexing her as I am vexed, daily, even as I compose this poem for you? do you know that I cannot dangle a cane such as this anywhere near my own pisiform, unlike Ellen?

[6] Glabella, noun – the smooth part of the forehead above & between the eyebrows

[7] Dorsum, noun – in the case of the nose, the tip

down to the abyss of the mental
eminence [8] where De Sousa
contrives an Aristotelian continuity
in the pattern of clothing below

    B. if I treat truly on Aurelia's philtrum, I fear
reprisals from beyond the pale

VI. Helene Schjerfbeck, 1912, verso, p. 340

    A. she is magnetized to my ice box door
since the last trip to Helsinki introducing
my son to his ersatz godmother, Emmy

    B. what of her philtrum? what of it

VII. Romaine Brooks, 1923, verso, p. 364

    A. swoon

    B. you have to get so incredibly close to
detect the potential for a philtrum

    C. how I respect

        a. the lines under her eyes

        b. her unimpeachable fashion

        c. the red suggestion of an
unrequited button hole

        d. pinprick eyes absolute are the
only gaze I need (& the only gaze
I could possibly stand [9])

        e. the bluest grey that has her back

VIII. Kathe Kollwitz, 1924, recto, p. 361

    A. so swollen it is convex

    B. suggestive of a blowfish in distress

    C. of the bloated consequences of
repressed speech

        i. inversely reflected in the tight
thin line of resignation that is her
penciled shadow mouth

        ii. ah but the as-above-so-below
parenthetical lines
circumscribing her dropped, gazing,
good left eye

---

[8] Mental eminence – told you already – see footer no. 6
- though I fear we do digress from our program now that into the femmes are we
  - o full sigh from nares nimble
  - o Aurelia would not be pleased, can't you tell?

[9] Re. a gaze, of any kind – it has been 3 ½ months / 15 weeks / 105 days since I have seen a live philtrum
- what gazing goes on goes on without
  - o whole quadrants of visage
  - o the vulnerabilities that render us invulnerable
  - o without a doubt without the kind of longing it's taken me so long to lick
  - o w/insufferable doubts it goes on, this gazing, without me

IX. Lee Krasner, 1931, verso, p. 366

                        A. close up w/out philtrum

X. Leonora Carrington 1937/1938, recto, p. 367

                        A. too far in middle distance to see a
                        philtrum

[10]

---

[10] This slatternly colloquy cannot hold me from the tongue
- it laps coarsely at the white roll above it (area that borders the top of the upper lip), searching for the sticky philtrum
    - o pushing back bile toward the isthmus of fauces while I give myself a medusa piercing w/out a mirror
        - waiting for the world to gyrate justly (once more?)

o

TRY THE GOAT

Valyntina Grenier

Amazon takes our minds off the forest the rain the taste
on the tongue rendering the most putrid fruit floral by design
Cattle with consequences like tweakers grind

hallucinogenic like when seagull suggests adventurous Virgil's garden
as a source eddies on the wind
Goats will try any angle

Increments do interesting things to animals
Arise toxify the goat Minimize
dangerous sustainable quantities of heightened powers humans allow to prove fatal

to figure somehow a single/ safe/ forbidden counterstrategy
animals intoxicate deliberately commonly
the sun eats its chromosomes explodes compounds mutates ultraviolet light prevents

       a caterpillar that leaves growing into butter trial and error
Photo synthesizers present species w/ a wild phosphorescent burn
Some plant paralyzer convulsive

and just caffeine unhinged w/ in
a nervous system kill drive
man-man predators stuffing their brains with visions to enslave our world
that time the same abominable mystery that dazzling arts brought even darker warfare
       poisons the vast chemical horrors atomized in protest

The Interview

Aaron Horwath

The sounds of friendly laughter that echoed from the depths of the office beyond the secretary's desk were the last thing Tim Wilkes wanted to hear as he sat waiting for the most important job interview of his life.

But before he even had a chance to close the magazine he had laid open across his lap, two men burst into the waiting area, their excited chatter and hand-shakes filling every inch of the room.

"...As I said, I could tell you were a Harvard man! You can't leave Harvard without catching a bit of that *je ne sais quoi*. My grandad and my son are both the same way," said one of the men, an older gentleman with speckled white hair and a fluffy beard who Tim assumed to be the hiring manager.

"Well, it would be an honor to work for a fellow Harvard man. I think we could do some truly special things," said the younger man. He wore a well-tailored, navy blue suit and shoes so polished they seemed to reflect every light particle in the lobby.

Tim watched the two men shake hands again, this time while holding the other's upper arm, embracing not as interviewer and interviewee, but instead like soon-to-be-inlaws. The younger man waved goodbye to the secretary who returned his pleasantry with a warm smile. As the younger man headed out towards the door, the older man made eye contact with Tim who sat with his closed magazine laying across his lap and his feet askew in a small lobby chair.

"You must be Tim," said the older man, extending a hand, "I am Andrew Buckley. Why don't you follow me back to my office?"

Mr. Buckly shook Tim's hand before leading him past the secretary's desk and through the lobby door. Tim tried to thank the secretary as he passed her desk—though he didn't know what for— but her eyes remained locked on the computer screen.

An awkward silence fell over the men as Mr. Buckley led Tim down a long hallway. Tim tried to appear distracted by admiring the pictures of smiling employees plastered along the length of the wall, each picture frame fitted with a small gold plate at the bottom that read *Employee of the Month.*

Tim considered making an innocuous comment about the pictures on the wall to break the silence, but before he could, he found himself being ushered into a large, but mostly empty, office. Once inside, Mr. Buckley took his place in a leather chair behind a large office desk while motioning for Tim to take a seat in a smaller office chair across from him.

For a few moments, Mr. Buckley fished around in a filing cabinet before pulling Tim's resume out of a drawer and placing it on the desk for both of them to see.

"Tim, thank you for coming by," Mr. Buckley began, "I thought you had an interesting resume and thought it would be good for us to talk."

"No, thank you, Mr. Buckley. It's a great opportunity and I appreciate you bringing me in."

"Absolutely, absolutely. And, really, call me Andrew," said Mr. Buckley, clasping his hands in front of him on the desk, "let's go back in time a bit. I see that you have a Bachelor's degree in Statistics and Mathematical Analysis and a Masters in International Business, is that correct?

"Yes...Andrew..." Tim said, hesitating to refer to Mr. Buckley by his first name, "I received both degrees from Cornell. They were wonderful programs and truly challenged me both intellectually and as a person. I think the rigors of the program really helped me grow into who I am today," said Tim, impressing himself with his use of *rigors* and hoping Mr. Buckley had noticed.

"Call me Mr. Buckley if you would, Tim," said Mr. Buckley, before continuing, "you can't grow without challenges in life, that's for sure. And it looks like you have completed...is that six internships?"

"Yes, that is right. Nasa and Google my senior year of my undergraduate. After my graduate degree, I thought public service might be my calling so I did a six-month internship at the NSA and then one right after at the Federal Housing Administration. Since working at FHA, I completed two other internship programs to, you know, gain more relevant experience, but those were at smaller companies."

"I see...you are referring to your time at Uber and then, most recently, your resume says you were an intern at WeChat in Shanghai?"

"Yes. WeChat especially was a great experience. I love Chinese culture and have always wanted to learn to speak the language. Living there gave me the opportunity to become fluent fairly quickly. I have to say, I was sad when the internship ended."

Tim smiled at himself, not expecting for there to be an opportunity for him to shoehorn in his time working in China into the interview.

"Sounds like valuable, real-world experience," Mr. Buckley said, pausing for a moment as he stared down at the resume before continuing.

"Tim, can I be straight with you?"

"Um, yes, of course," Tim sputtered, surprised by Mr. Buckley's sudden change in tone.

"Here at Buckley Groceries, we don't provide just any old service. We are responsible for feeding our community and we do it with the freshest produce, the most ethical dairy, and the biggest smiles on our faces. We are the literal lifeblood of the neighborhood and we take great pride in that. It is our belief that to serve our community the right way, everyone, including our shelf-stockers, need to bring 100% of their heart and soul to the job every day. No exceptions."

"Yes, of course, Mr. Buckley, I would never bring anything less. I think my track record at other respectable companies certainly demonstrates that I have what it takes to excel as a shelf-stocker."

"You see," said Mr. Buckley, ignoring Tim's previous statement, "we need a shelf-stocker who is as precise with a box opener as a sushi chef is with his *Yanagi-ba*, someone who glides through the aisles like Tonya Harding, someone who arranges cartons of milk with the attention to detail and inspiration of Michelangelo hanging from the ceiling of the Sistine Chapel. For our ideal candidate, carrying boxes out from the loading bay and putting each item in its rightful place on the shelf is not merely a job, but a vocation, a calling of the highest order."

Mr. Buckley stopped and leaned back in his chair. Tim froze for a moment, trying to find the right words to assure Mr. Buckley he could live up to his lofty expectations and truly embody the dream employee Mr. Buckley described.

"I can assure you Mr. Buckley," started Tim, "if given the opportunity, no box will go unopened, no barcode un-scanned, no-spill un-mopped on my watch. I truly believe this is the job that life has spent nearly four decades preparing me for."

"I know Tim, I can see it in your eyes. And I admire that. But I have to say, I am worried about your experience. For a position like this, we like to see *at least* eight internships and a few years of industry experience if possible."

Tim could hear the interview, and the opportunity, slipping away from him in the tone of Mr. Buckey's voice.

"I can assure you that my grit and hard work can make up for whatever experience I might lack, Mr. Buckley," stammered Tim.

With his arms crossed and leaning as far back as his chair would allow, Mr. Buckley ran his eyes up and down Tim.

"I am sure it could Tim. Listen, I appreciate you coming in. We will email you about our selection in the next week or so."

Before Tim realized it, he had stood up and was shaking hands with Mr. Buckley while being escorted out of his office. At the door to the lobby, they said goodbye and shook hands again.

"You seem like a smart cookie," said Mr. Buckley, "I assume you can find your way out. Just walk past the janitor's closet, out through the dairy section, and take a right at produce, just the way you came in. Thank you again for coming by Tim."

Tim shook Mr. Buckley's hand once more before stepping out of the lobby. As he had when he arrived, he made his way through the dairy aisle, then past customers smelling mangos and examining brussel sprouts, before exiting Buckley's Groceries through a pair of automatic sliding glass doors that *whooshed* as they opened.

Outside the entrance to the store, his mother's van sat idling along the curb, white smoke coming from the tailpipe in the cool, early-winter weather. He knocked on the passenger window, waiting for the familiar sounds of the unlocking doors before pulling on the door handle.

"Hey sweetie how did things go?" said his mother as she took her reading glasses from her nose and placed her book in the van's center console.

"I don't know. Not great. It looked like the guy walking out when I was waiting in the lobby nailed the interview," Tim said as he slid into the passenger's seat, "and the hiring manager said he was worried about my lack of experience."

Tim waited for a comforting response from his mother, but after hundreds of interviews and as many rejections, she hardly had any comforting words left to give. A few moments of silence passed before Tim spoke again.

"Hey, mom?"

"Yes?"

"Do you think we can go get some ice cream?"

"Sure honey," his mother said as she shifted the van into drive, "you deserve a treat after your big interview. But you need to buckle up your seatbelt before we can go."

The Truth About Aging

Phoebe Tsang

I found my first grey hair at twenty-seven. That year I pulled out at least a dozen, staring in the mirror in my boyfriend's basement bedroom at his parents' house.

My boyfriend was a jazz drummer, and jazz jams usually start around midnight. Most mornings, I crawled back to the basement alone while he was still crushing caffeinated renditions of Cole Porter ballads.

One afternoon, we woke to drops of cold water splashing on our faces. The ground-floor toilet tank had cracked and flooded, after his father over-tightened the mounting bolts. Years of band practice in the room directly below had shaken the screws loose, and the tank was starting to detach from the toilet bowl.

If my boyfriend wasn't a drummer, we wouldn't have been rudely awakened by waste water.

For six months after the breakup I combed my hair obsessively, scouring my scalp for the first signs of grey among the black. I found nothing.

Ever since my twenty-seventh year, I've been on edge. Discipline and self-control are my defence. Failure at times is unavoidable, and the enemy takes root. When that happens, I remind myself I'm only human. Then I reach for my tweezers.

Years can go by without incident when out of the blue, a silver sprout. Sometimes, a closer look at the root reveals that the hair has gone back to growing in black. I choose forgiveness, and strengthen my resolve to avoid Clairol at all costs.

As for the red, blonde, and copper strands: I don't know where they come from—changes in diet, a shift in hormones, or Mongolian ancestors. I let them be. They're my lucky streaks.

My brush with greying has taught me to make the most of however long I have left. Who knows when the end will come? So far, my mane can't rival Rapunzel's, but she had an early start (stolen at birth, locked in a tower). I wear mine in a fishtail braid, wound thrice round my waist like a girdle, or as a neck warmer. When I feel like going the extra mile, I build a beehive pompadour worthy of Marie Antoinette's head.

I'm fifty-five years old, and my hair has never looked better. Glossy and dark, with subtle highlights. People stop me in the street, and ask where I go to get such natural-looking colour. When I tell them my secret, they don't believe me.

It's been more than twenty-seven years since I woke with sewage on my face, but you can't be too careful. I rise early and am in bed by midnight. I avoid basements, and always inspect a bathroom's plumbing before I flush. If jazz comes on the radio, I switch channels. I've slipped up and gone on a few dates that I know I'll regret in the morning, as soon as I look in the mirror. Most of the time, I'd rather stay home and wash my hair.

Recently, I met a guy who could be The One. He's an accountant who works from home, in a penthouse condo bought with the money he saved as a student while his peers were out partying. He only listens to classical music, and both his parents are dead.

Perhaps my luck has finally caught up with me.

Starting a new relationship will be a huge risk, but I'm ready. Change can happen overnight, or you can slow it down.

Astrologers call your twenty-seventh year a Saturn return, and a lot of people don't make it. Jimi Hendrix, Janis Joplin, and Amy Winehouse all died at twenty-seven. And not just because of jazz.

I told my soon-to-be-boyfriend what my real age is, and he thinks I'm joking. Even though there's no way my hair could be this long if I was really twenty-seven, like him. (He thinks it's extensions.)

The other day, he found his first grey strand. I asked him what he was going to do about it, and he said it didn't bother him. He explained that his father was bald by his age, so he has nothing to complain about.

I may be old enough to be his mother, but I can't shield him from the truth forever. It's time I let my hair down.

Therapy Session

Art by Bill Schulz
Poetry by Paul Benkendorfer

What are thoughts but memories lurking in the abstract?
      Voices form from the shadows like lines of tangled webs
The boy sits in silence; timid and confused
      The demons call from the recesses of the psyche
The bald therapist looks on in deep contemplation
      Faces emerge through the trenches of the mind
What do you see? he asks the boy
      Young eyes stare vacantly outward
I can barely make them out, he says. The demons.
      The bearded face of a man along with three youths form-sneering
The therapist asks the boy to go on
      Their hands emerge through the haze of thought
The boy rubs his cheek
      The sting of a slap fresh on his face
The boy returns to sitting in solemn silence
      The faces merge into contorted forms
They haunt me, says the boy. They won't leave me alone.
      Their mocking laughter echoes in his mind, maniacally.
The boy now lost with the ghosts ingrained in his subconscious
      The vision clearer now, the faces materialize--his father and brothers
Their harsh words bombard him like so many blows
      "Stupid", "fat", "Worthless", "Waste of space"
The boy looks on blankly and the therapist asks what else
      But there is nothing; only silence remains

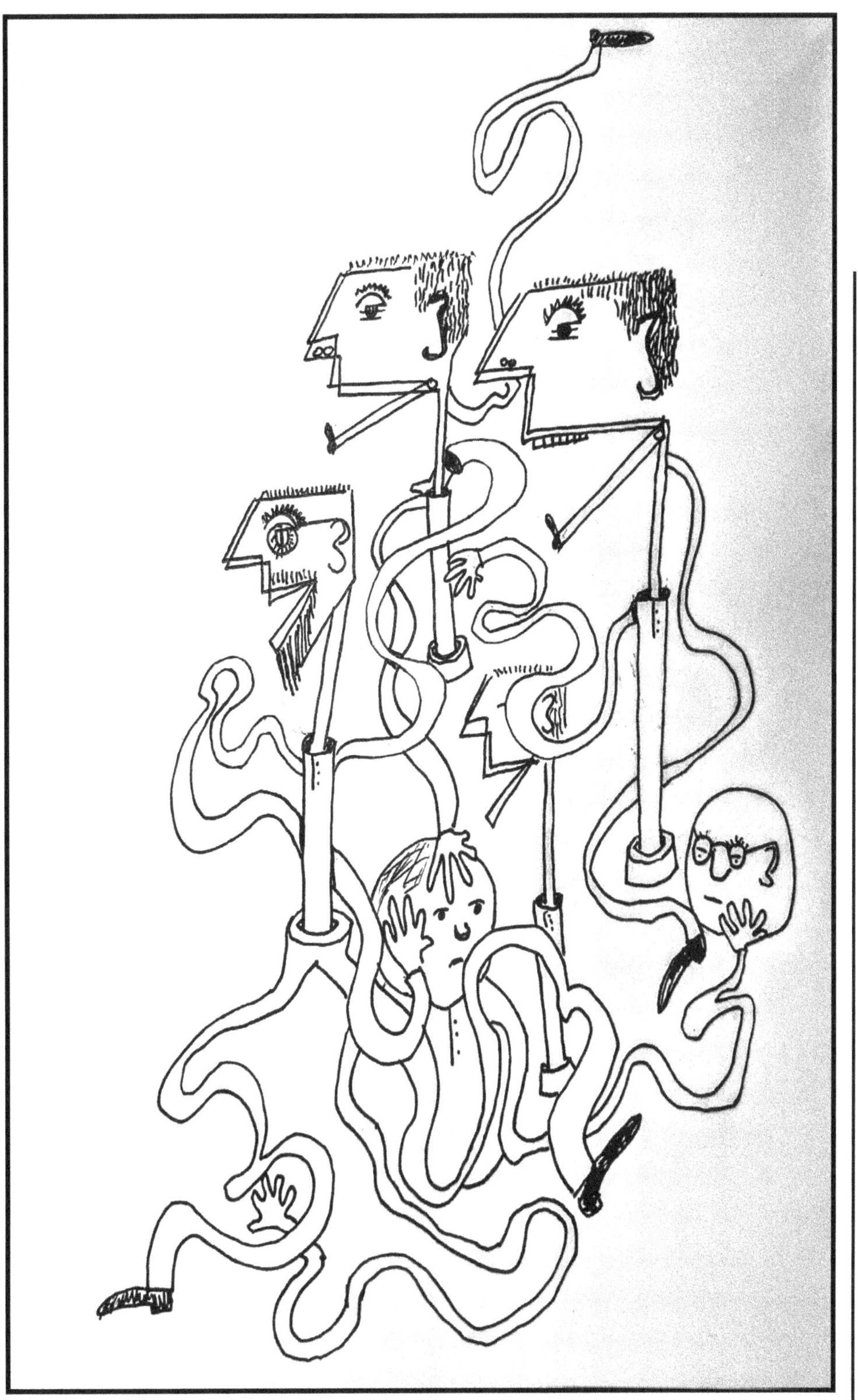

In Order Of Appearance:

Tom Halford lives in Corner Brook, NL with his wife and kids. He is a teacher at Grenfell Campus, Memorial University of Newfoundland.

Matt Gold is based in Brooklyn, NY, where he divides his time between music and photography. As evidence of the democratizing nature of his approach to photography, Gold has no formal training in the visual arts. His first image, a picture of his cat on a Sony Ericsson Z310A flip phone, was taken in 2008, and he has continued to explore the aesthetic possibilities of that instrument. Gold's work has been featured in numerous publications and journals.

Jeff lives in a New Jersey town so small it has no traffic lights, and only one craft brewery. His writing has garnered positive notices and unusual prizes, such as winning a trip to a Red Hot Chili Peppers concert, or a decorative pillow. He finished his first play in 2020.

Adele Evershed writes prose and poetry inbetween trying to educate her family to take up the items on the bottom step with them when they go upstairs. Both activities involve a great deal of hope in the face of bitter experience! Adele has had her poetry published by Three Drops from a Cauldron and Didcot Writers. She will also have poems in the up and coming anthologies, Southwest Poetry Review, The Whitman Collaboration Project, and Winter 2020 published by Other Worldly Women Press. Adele's flash fiction can be found in a number of online publications including Every Day Fiction and Reflex Fiction among others.

Bordnick, an Industrial design graduate of Pratt Institute in New York. He have been a designer and design director for the past twenty years including for numerous company, corporate and government projects. They included a children's museum, for the city of New York and the Board of Education, involved in all aspects of marketing and design. jackbordnickstudio.com

Marco Buttice is a literature maven and freelance writer from Montreal, Quebec. His work has been published in The Void Magazine, Soliloquies Anthology, and more. You can usually find him eating a large plate of pasta or binging a Netflix Original Series, perhaps at the same time.

Heather Gluck is a New York poet whose work deals in all things visceral, unresolved, and alive. She's been published most recently in Cathexis Northwest Press, Beyond Words, and Some Kind of Opening, and she was named 2nd place in the 2021 Tennessee Williams Writing Contest. Heather is currently completing an MFA at Columbia University.

Marla McFadin is a psychotherapist currently living and working in Eugene, Oregon. She grew up in the 1970s and 1980s in a small-ish town near the coast in California, reading, reading, reading. She wants to recover the dreaming world from her adulthood.

Joanna Baxter is a multidisciplinary artist and creative entrepreneur based in Vancouver, British Columbia. She is a graduate of SFU's The Writers Studio and the co-host of a quarterly reader event, "SPiEL". Across a variety of media, Baxter explores the private and public absurdities of social construct. Instagram: @avoiding.the.elephant

Martha Clarkson's writing and photography can be found in monkeybicycle, F-Stop, Clackamas Literary Review, Seattle Review, Portland Review, Black Box Gallery, Tulane Review, Mothering Magazine,, Feminine Rising, and Nimrod. She has two notable short stories in Best American Short Stories. www.marthaclarkson.com

Chase Ferree (he/him) is a teacher in Seattle, WA. Originally from North Carolina, he's also lived in Missouri and Massachusetts. His poems have appeared or are forthcoming in Emerge Literary Journal, Peripheries Journal, Perhappened, Horse Egg Literary, and elsewhere.

Beth Curran has been teaching English for twenty-two years. Her poetry focuses on the mysteries and everyday wonders of being a woman, wife, mother, and New England girl at heart. For the past few summers, she has been attending the Conference on Poetry and Teaching at The Frost Place, tucked away in the mountains in Franconia, New Hampshire, where she served as their 2019 Schafer Teaching Fellow. Her poetry has appeared in Tiny Seed Literary Journal, The Write Launch, High Shelf Press, and forthcoming in The Worcester Review. Her work has also been featured in the Wickford Art Association's annual Poetry and Art Exhibition in Rhode Island. She resides in Jacksonville, Florida with her family. Instagram: gansettgirlwrites

Alina Stefanescu was born in Romania and lives in Birmingham, Alabama with her partner and several intense mammals. Her writing can be found in diverse journals, including Prairie Schooner, North American Review, FLOCK, Southern Humanities Review, Crab Creek Review, Up the Staircase Quarterly, Virga, Whale Road Review, and others. She serves as Poetry Editor for Pidgeonholes, Co-Director of PEN America's Birmingham Chapter, Co-Founder of 100,000 Poets for Change Birmingham, and proud board member of Magic City Poetry Festival. She was nominated for 5 Pushcart Prizes by various journals in 2019. A finalist for the 2019 Kurt Brown AWP Prize, Alina won the 2019 River Heron Poetry Prize. She still can't believe (or deserve) any of this. More online at www.alinastefanescuwriter.com.

Connor Doyle is an emerging photographer and filmmaker based in the Chicagoland area. Using a number of analog film formats, Doyle's work focuses on the idiosyncratic details of daily life in the Northern Illinois. Though often trivial, his subjects capture the formal beauty and potency of these everyday sites, urging his viewers to reflect on the significance of their lived experiences. Doyle's work has been featured in Hampshire College's The Reader, the Prairie Light Review, and The Hole In The Head Review.

Dig Wayne grew up in Ohio. He has lived and worked in New York City and London. He now lives in Los Angles. He has been a poet and photographer as long as he can remember. His poerty has been featured in the literary jounals, Askew, Spillway and others. The only god he prays to is Thelonious Monk. As Monk states: "There ain't no wrong notes on the piano." Dig teaches Method Acting at the Lee Strasberg Theatre Institute in West Hollywood. digwayne.com

Lauren Kalita is a writer and artist living on Cape Cod. Her writing has been published in two of Columbia University's journals, and she had poetry readings at the iconic West End Bar in New York City in the early aughts. More recently two of her poems were featured in Quaranzine of the Wellfleet Public Library. Her photographs have been hung at Columbia's LeRoy Neiman gallery, as well as at Cotuit Center for the Arts, the Cultural Center of Cape Cod, the Arts Foundation of Cape Cod, the Cape Cod Museum of Art, Plymouth Center for the Arts (where one of her photos took an honorable mention), and Attleboro Art Museum. Lauren completed a residency with the Cordial Eye Gallery during the summer of 2020, for which she made 15 assemblages, began the feral women photographic series, and composed 15 new poems for her Slit project, exploring what it is to slit and be slit as a woman. Lauren was invited to exhibit at the Creative Hands Gallery in late 2020, and in 2021 she will have poems and photographs in the Mutual Muses show at the Cultural Center of Cape Cod.

Valyntina Grenier is an LGBTQIA+ multi-genre artist living in Tucson, Arizona. Her tête-bêche chapbook Fever Dream / Take Heart, was published by Cathexis Northwest Press, January 2020. Find her at valyntinagrenier.com or Insta @valyntinagrenier

Aaron Horwath is an American expat having spent the last five years living in both Vietnam and The Netherlands. When he isn't writing, he can be found nose-deep in the pages of Emerson, Kafka, and F. Scott Fitzgerald. His other short stories can be found published at Across the Margin and From Whispers to Roars.

Phoebe Tsang is a Hong-Kong born Chinese, British and Canadian poet, author, librettist and playwright, and the author of 'Contents of a Mermaid's Purse' (Tightrope Books, Toronto). Her poetry and fiction has been published internationally in anthologies and journals including Asia Literary Review, Literary Review of Canada, The Bombay Review, Geist, and Room Magazine. Her libretti have been commissioned and premiered by orchestras and ensembles including the Toronto Symphony Orchestra, Hamilton Philharmonic, and Tapestry Opera. www.phoebetsang.com.

Bill Schulz lives in Windham, Maine. He is a poet, photographer, and manic doodler. His poetry and artwork have appeared in may periodicals over the past 40 years, including The Aurorean,

High Shelf, Seneca Review, and Nine Mile.

Paul Benkendorfer is an AP English teacher from Queen Creek, Arizona. As an educator Paul has worked extensively with at-risk and special needs youth for close to a decade. Paul attended the University of Arizona in Tucson where he received his Bachelor's in Creative Writing. In 2020, Paul earned his Master's in Teaching Writing from The Johns Hopkins University with a focus on how writing can be used to help at-risk youth develop their academic skills and overcome trauma. Paul's work has been featured in several anthologies, journals, and magazines including High Shelf Press, Eerie River Publishing, Black Hare Press, The Write Launch, Allegory Ridge, the Dark Poet's Club as well as many others.

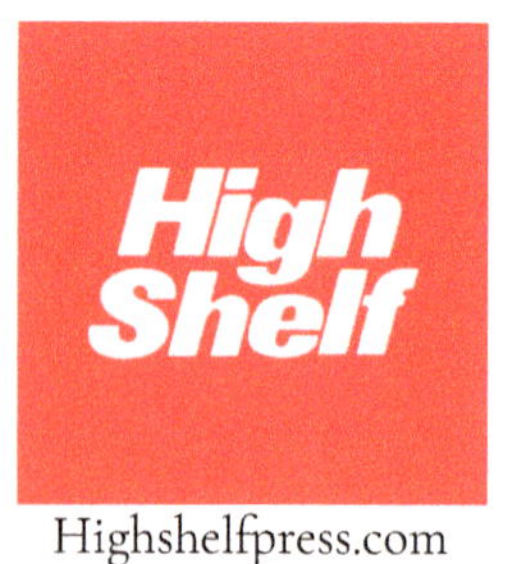

Highshelfpress.com